THE

PSYCHIC

WORKBOOK

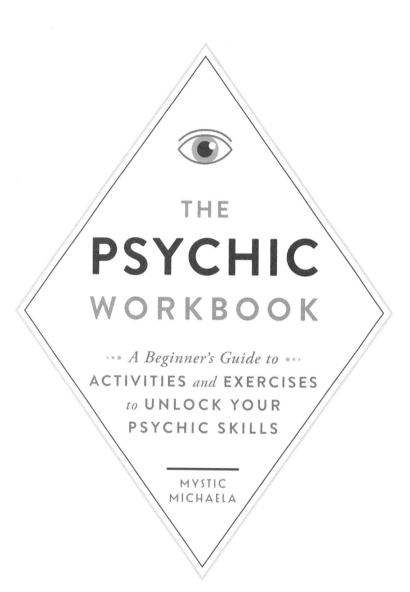

THE
PSYCHIC
WORKBOOK

A Beginner's Guide to
ACTIVITIES *and* EXERCISES
to UNLOCK YOUR
PSYCHIC SKILLS

MYSTIC
MICHAELA

ADAMS MEDIA
NEW YORK LONDON TORONTO SYDNEY NEW DELHI

Adams Media
An Imprint of Simon & Schuster, Inc.
100 Technology Center Drive
Stoughton, Massachusetts 02072

First Adams Media trade paperback edition January 2023

ADAMS MEDIA and colophon are trademarks of Simon & Schuster.

For information about special discounts for bulk purchases, please contact Simon & Schuster Special Sales at 1-866-506-1949 or business@simonandschuster.com.

The Simon & Schuster Speakers Bureau can bring authors to your live event. For more information or to book an event contact the Simon & Schuster Speakers Bureau at 1-866-248-3049 or visit our website at www.simonspeakers.com.

Interior design by Colleen Cunningham
Images © 123RF/bravissimos; Getty Images/kpp; Simon & Schuster, Inc.

Manufactured in the United States of America

2 2023

ISBN 978-1-5072-2020-7

*To the
Mystic Michaela
Spiritual
Family.*

Author's Note

Being psychic is about love. The love you display for others when you help a person connect to their inner truths, the love you feel on the other side when you receive messages, and, most of all, the love you feel for yourself when you allow Spirit to speak to you through your psychic gifts. Growing up in a psychic family, I was fortunate enough to be handed down generational lessons about what it means to connect with Spirit. And the main lesson I learned is that it's about love.

My goal for this book is to lay the foundation for you to begin the beautiful journey of strengthening your unique psychic abilities. In this book, I have set out the methods I have used to connect with Spirit over the years. I have provided detailed descriptions of the psychic paths I have discovered while navigating my own journey to connect with this other-worldly realm. There will be many lessons upon the road, but always remembering that it starts with you will be your ever-lasting light as you travel. Using this workbook to get back to the most important element of your practice, yourself, will be a valuable touchstone. Take care with yourself, feel gratitude for this energy you are about to receive, and, most of all, remember to feel the love.

Contents

Introduction

15

How to Use This Workbook

17

••• *Part 1* •••

Understanding Your Psychic Abilities

19

What Does It Mean to Be Psychic?

21

Who Is Sending These Messages?

23

The Six "Clairs"

27

Tapping Into Intuition

30

Getting Ready to Use Your Psychic Abilities

34

••• *Part 2* •••

Psychic Workbook Exercises
39

Activity 1
Open Your Third Eye
41

Activity 2
Perform an Energy Scan of Your Environment
46

Activity 3
Sense Someone Else's Feelings
51

Activity 4
Create a Protection Bubble
56

Activity 5
Balance Your Chakras
61

Activity 6
Connect with the Earth
67

Activity 7
Interpret Your Dreams
72

Activity 8
Meet One of Your Spirit Guides
77

Activity 9
Create a Spirit Guide Symbol Book
82

Activity 10
Practice Remote Viewing
87

Activity 11
Look for Auras
92

Activity 12
Hear the World Beyond
98

Activity 13
Develop Your Clear Smelling
103

Activity 14
Send a Telepathic Text
108

Activity 15
Channel Spirit in Your Art
113

Activity 16
Channel Spirit in Writing
118

Activity 17
Manifest an Intention
124

Activity 18
Choose a Crystal for Psychic Work
130

Activity 19
Read a Picture's Energy
135

Activity 20
Receive Messages from Objects
141

Activity 21
Do a Palm Reading
146

Activity 22
Program a Crystal
151

Activity 23
Receive Messages from Ancestral Photos
156

Activity 24
Use Your Psychic Calendar
161

Activity 25
Astral Project with Purpose
166

Activity 26

Discover an Animal Messenger

172

Activity 27

Perform a House Cleansing and Blessing

177

Activity 28

Test Your Long-Term Psychic Predictions

182

Activity 29

Investigate Paranormal Activity

187

Activity 30

Assign Colors to a Situation

192

Activity 31

Interpret Your Angel Numbers

197

Activity 32

Send Someone Away Energetically

202

Activity 33

Communicate with Pets

207

Activity 34

Get In Touch with the Moon

212

Activity 35

Connect to Past Lives

217

Activity 36

Organize and Use Mystical Protection Tools

222

Activity 37

Remove Negative Attachments

228

Activity 38

Visualize the Immediate Future

233

Activity 39

Psychically Interpret Handwriting

238

Activity 40

Understand and Shift Your Energy

243

Index

249

Introduction

You are psychic and always have been. You were born with the ability to perceive the world around you in an energetic way! Everything has energy; objects, people, events, and places all give off a frequency. And fine-tuning your ability to interpret these frequencies is what strengthening your innate psychic abilities is all about. With motivation and an open mind, you can begin to read between the lines of the world around you and take a closer look at your inner thoughts. In doing so, you'll gain insight into yourself *and* your life, and boost your ability to communicate, interpret situations, and even connect others to the incredible worlds beyond.

The Psychic Workbook is your guide to unlocking your natural abilities! In Part 1, you'll find out exactly what it means to be a psychic, and who (or what) is speaking to you through the messages you receive. You'll also explore the connection between intuition and psychic abilities, the six "clairs" used by successful psychics, and obstacles that may try to get in the way of your powers. You will learn how to come to terms with your own fear and self-doubt and how to center yourself in a calm and focused state of mind so that you can maximize your psychic talents.

After laying the groundwork for psychic practice, you will discover forty step-by-step activities designed to help you strengthen aspects of your psychic abilities and take care of yourself and your needs along the way. You'll:

- ✦ Receive messages from ancestral photos.
- ✦ Balance your chakras.
- ✦ Send a telepathic text.
- ✦ Connect to past lives.
- ✦ Create a protection bubble to manage the energies around you.
- ✦ And so much more.

These activities will set you up for a lifetime of psychic growth, because your journey doesn't end when you finish this book.

Learning about how you are psychic, and nurturing those skills, will be different from anyone else's psychic journey. Why? Because *you* are the key to understanding the unique way you interpret energy. You will be journeying inward and becoming closer to yourself than ever before. With the lessons and exercises in this book, you will see the universe in a whole new way. Get ready for an amazing adventure; divine shifts are underway in your life!

How to Use This Workbook

Welcome to the mystical domain of the psychic! The subtle ways you are about to dive into your subconscious are going to change your perspective and ways of thinking. This book will assist you on the path to developing your psychic abilities and help you keep track of your progress so that you can revisit different moments and renew principal skills whenever necessary.

In Part 1 of this workbook, you will learn about how you are already equipped with the tools necessary to be psychic. With more attention to your own senses, emotions, and daily routines, you will begin to understand those tools and activate their reception to energetic messages in the world around you—and within yourself. You will uncover the ties between intuition and being psychic and learn how to tap into your intuition effectively. Finally, you will explore the steps for starting your own psychic journey: setting an intention and meditating prior to a psychic practice. This section includes steps for meditating, as well as a full meditation script you can follow before each activity in Part 2, to clear your mind and focus on the skill you are about to perform. You may decide to use this script when beginning your journey, then adapt it or try a different meditation technique later, once you are more solid in your psychic abilities.

In Part 2, forty easy-to-follow exercises will use your natural inclination toward reading energy to help you grow your psychic gifts. Some exercises focus on developing a specific sense or emotional intuition, while others explore a popular method of divining spirit messages, such as palm reading or interpreting angel numbers. There are also exercises designed to help you care for yourself along this journey. Changing your perception and opening yourself up to the energies and messages beyond physical reality can feel overwhelming, even exhausting at times. The self-care activities in Part 2 are an important part of recharging your mind, body, and soul so that you can go into the next psychic practice feeling renewed and ready to enhance your skills.

Each activity is organized so that you will:

1. Learn more about theme(s) of being psychic.
2. Discover how to get started in doing the activity.
3. Find step-by-step instructions for doing the activity.
4. Try it out for yourself and write about your experience.

When reflecting on how an activity went, be descriptive and thoughtful about what you experienced. You can answer each of the provided questions, answer those that resonate with you, or use them as inspiration for your personal reflection.

Do the first five exercises first and pay particularly close attention to them. These are foundational practices that will be a basis for the others. After you feel comfortable with those initial activities, feel free to flip through to whatever activities catch your eye and complete them in any order you choose.

This is a lifelong adventure you are about to embark on; there is no rush to complete every activity or master a particular skill as soon as possible. As you will see, the reward lies within you when you discover just how powerful you truly are. With this book, you will find a peaceful place to relish your psychic connection.

Part 1

Understanding Your Psychic Abilities

When anyone describes their own psychic abilities, they are coming at it from a personal point of view. To be psychic, you really must first understand how you are uniquely attuned to receiving psychic messages from unseen realms. There are fundamentals to becoming psychic, and as you tap into them you can better realize the nuances in which divine messengers, ancestors, and other voices speak to you. As you better acquaint yourself with these psychic building blocks, you will learn how to hone your intuition and ability to discern messages from the noise of your thoughts.

In this part, you will explore how to use your existing senses to heighten your psychic abilities, as well as how your own emotions and desires bring meaning and power into the divine practices you employ. The ever-present voice of self-doubt will also be explained and repurposed so that you can learn to use it without letting it hinder your confidence when practicing psychic skills. Then you will learn about how centering yourself in meditation before each psychic practice will eventually make connecting to the universe feel like second nature to you. Here you will find easy-to-follow steps and a helpful meditation script to use before trying the different activities in Part 2.

WHAT DOES IT MEAN TO BE PSYCHIC?

When people hear the word "psychic," a myriad of preconceived notions flood their minds. Many times, the moment this gift is mentioned, it is dismissed as nonsense, dark, or a creative trick with smoke and mirrors. For this reason, the idea of what it means to be psychic is one you will have to at first reconstruct in your own mind, shedding common misunderstandings for the truth: Being psychic means connecting yourself and others to the limitless source of unconditional love and universe energy. The links that can be forged via your own compassion, knowledge, and good intentions are priceless for those who wish to find connection, comfort, and closure. Being a psychic signifies being a helper, a healer, and a communicator. You are a conduit of messages for yourself and others from the universe and Spirit.

The term "universe" encompasses all the potential and limitless abundance available to everyone. It is the pool of endless knowledge that we are all a part of and, therefore, can tap into in order to align our goals with the goals of nature itself. When we talk about manifesting intentions, or the currents of energy that we are all swept up in, "universe" is the term often used. Meanwhile, "Spirit" is the intelligent and more individualized voice that connects to you specifically, bringing you divine messages that can alter your life's trajectory. This can be a cover-all term for spirit guides, ancestors, your Higher Self, and loved ones on the other side. When suddenly seeing a vision that connects you to a friend, or receiving a message linked to a person you are close to, it is Spirit who is communicating with you. However, keep in mind that you may use whatever terms you feel comfortable with moving forward. There are countless names for the powers larger than us all.

The Psychic's Intention

Preparing to expand your own psychic sense—your own abilities to help, heal, and communicate—begins with your intention. Having a set intention for why you want to develop and strengthen this precious gift, in addition to the understanding of what it truly means to be psychic, is going to help you in combating the narrow-minded assessments others may have. If you truly understand why you want to do this, you will know deep down that this intention, or higher consciousness goal, is something you can support.

Wanting to connect telepathically to a friend in need; understanding the meaning behind an object that brings you joy, sadness, or mystery; or wanting to provide closure for yourself with a loved one who has passed are all intentions that you may establish before embarking on a psychic task. Setting your intention in this positive light will assist you in maintaining confidence while honing your natural-born gift, and it will set the tone in a great way as you take the first steps along your journey of being psychic.

Psychic Skills and Intuition

Have you ever had a sudden feeling that something was totally off? Perhaps you just knew your friend's new boyfriend wasn't good for her, or that a coworker was stealing from the register? You may not have known why you felt that way, but you couldn't shake it. This is your intuition.

Intuition is an innate intelligence that everyone has. It's your honing beacon of sorts—the internal messaging center to the universe itself. Everyone and everything emit vibrations all the time. No matter what words or actions they are presenting outwardly, there is a feeling of disconnect you can gather. Your Higher Self is the part of you that exists between worlds, and your intuition is the voice of that self. This portion of who you are is communicating to give you the truth that lies in whatever is left unspoken.

In many professions, intuition is something that is celebrated and encouraged, like a doctor who intuitively knows what to do in a critical moment during surgery or a stockbroker who intuitively sees a good investment before anyone else can. The ability to read beyond superficial cues is a skill that with time and energy can be enhanced.

All psychic skills take intuition. They also utilize it in interpreting the messages gleaned during a psychic practice. Picking up on someone in a more alert and conscious way can create the bridge from your natural intuition to a fully developed psychic ability. Psychic skills are the leveling up of intuition for the purpose of delivering messages, connecting to the other side, and predicting what will happen moving forward. Your psychic skills are in fact an intuitive ability.

Later in this chapter, you will discover more about intuition and how it will shape your psychic journey, including obstacles to be mindful of and how exactly you can tune in to and hone your intuition. As you read on in Part 1, intuition will be further explored.

WHO IS SENDING THESE MESSAGES?

The messages you will be tapping into during your psychic practices will come from a few different sources. These unique voices you will become familiar with have distinct variations. Becoming used to mindfully reflecting upon how the thoughts in your mind present themselves, how they make you feel, and how they enter your field of comprehension will allow you to differentiate them. The following are different sources of psychic messages.

Spirit Guides and Angels

Spirit guides, or angels, are your high-vibrational team of beings who personally watch and aid in your every move. These beings are consistently trying to communicate with you through symbols, numbers, and people you meet. Their job is to nudge you along to reach certain points on your existing soul contract (a kind of to-do list your Higher Self created before you began this lifetime). You will be able to communicate and get messages from your spirit guides, as well as from other peoples' guides, when you tap into your psychic senses.

The voice spirit guides use to speak with you has a peaceful yet powerful tone to it. It comes in fast, as it's often the first voice you'll hear when you begin to pay attention, and with a surprising neutrality. It is a feeling of truth and peace. It enters without fanfare, more like a silent knowing. It's the voice telling you to apply for the new job you just saw or introduce yourself to the interesting stranger you just made eye contact with. It's a voice that often challenges you, which feels in your best interest, yet also is an observation of what you do. It does not stay or persist. It arrives quietly, presents itself, and washes over you.

The Higher Self

As you learned previously in this chapter, your Higher Self is the part of you that coexists between this realm and the next. It is your soul's true identity—the eternal you that you have always been and will always go back to. This is the part of you that is your knowing. It is your natural intuitive self that you can look back upon and realize you may have heard but shut out. Think of this earth plane as a classroom for advanced spiritual healing and learning and your Higher Self as the teacher.

When you develop your psychic sense, you will be able to sense the Higher Self of others. This part of them is sometimes very different from the persona they are presenting. You can feel the disconnect between what they say and who they are when their Higher Self tries to step out from the shadow that the person has cast it in.

The voice of your Higher Self feels intuitively your own. It lives within you and comes from inside. It feels very familiar to you—like the best version of you. It's positive and uplifting. It can often see the bigger picture and identify the lessons behind what is going on currently in your life.

Loved Ones on the Other Side

During your psychic practices, you may also come into contact with those who have passed. These could be your own ancestors, those you have personally known in life, or even loved ones of people you are doing psychic readings for. Energies such as this will feel as if you are getting someone else's thoughts, words, or opinions. They can feel a bit nagging or persistent, as if you have to do something right now. They often require action. You may also get visions that are not your own, that feel borrowed.

Spirit Shivers

One physical, telltale sign you will get when receiving a profound message from Spirit or your Higher Self is through "spirit shivers." A spirit shiver is a special kind of feeling—one you may have gotten at other times in your life without understanding what it's for or about. It can start at the crown of your head, or sometimes in the center of your body, and spread out warmly. Physically, it feels like a mix between goosebumps and a shiver running through you.

People can experience spirit shivers when something "resonates," meaning, they hear something that permeates deep into their soul. This can happen during psychic readings, deep conversations with friends, and when realizing something for the first time in a very profound way. As you begin to acknowledge spirit shivers, they will occur more often.

The Ego Voice

The ego voice is the human part of you that is sending messages. It is not the same as your Higher Self voice because it is rooted solely in the physical world. This voice is often the loudest, yet it's actually never the first voice to speak to you. It follows the voices of Spirit, loved ones on the other side, angels, spirit guides or other ascended beings, and your Higher Self. This is the voice that will downplay an accomplishment or brush off something that felt like a connection. It is usually the same pessimistic, doubtful, and fearful voice that follows any intuitive thought. Deciding whether to pay attention to the message of your ego voice will depend on the situation. But you will always have to acknowledge it. Understanding what your ego voice is telling you to do and why will create an extra layer of insight and control in your psychic abilities. Later in this chapter, you will learn about the purpose of the ego and how it impacts intuition. In Part 2, you will find advice for checking in on your ego voice during activities that may tempt it to speak up.

The Creative Voice

Within your mind is a whirl of thoughts, ideas, and connections. Your mind is always moving, creating, and reacting to the world around you. Because of this, part of your psychic journey will be learning the difference between your creative voice and the messages you are receiving from Spirit or your Higher Self. At first, it's very easy to mix psychic messages up with your imagination. You may create a feeling in your mind that turns out to be simply your imagination coming up with ideas. Your creative voice can also be influenced by what you watch, see, or are currently dealing with in your own life.

You will find that your creative voice is colorful, a bit hyper, and loud, kind of like the voice of a child. It will communicate in random outbursts that seem connected to something you've already been doing or something you want to happen. As you perform the exercises in Part 2, you will learn to subtract your creative voice from the psychic messages you receive. It takes time and patience, as well as lots of reflective practice, but once you learn to do this, it will enhance your psychic craft.

THE SIX "CLAIRS"

Tapping into the messages sent to you from beyond the physical realm will open up a whole new world of senses to you. Society teaches you to respond and respect your five physical senses: hearing, sight, taste, touch, and smell. And these are an important tool in understanding the world. However, there are a few "updates" to this elementary knowledge you'll need to know to move forward on your psychic journey. These updates are the psychic senses and every bit as real and tangible as their physical counterparts. Through the psychic senses, your physical senses expand to accommodate sensing not just this earth plane but also what lies beyond. You are a conduit for spirit activity, and Spirit will use your existing human functions like the five senses to show what you need to know.

The psychic senses will be essential to honing your abilities as a psychic, and you will see each of them come up within activities in Part 2 of this book.

Clairvoyance

Have you ever seen a brush of color around someone that wasn't tangible, or had an image pop into your mind's eye so strongly it felt foreign? Clairvoyance is "clear seeing"; this is your ability to "see" visuals from the past, present, and future with either your physical eyes or your third eye. They are given to you to by Spirit either as a certain message, validation and a show of solidarity with the forces larger than you, or to enhance a life experience. Over time, you will know the difference between simple imagination and your "clear sight" vision. Many activities in Part 2 will employ your clairvoyant vision, such as "Open Your Third Eye," "Meet One of Your Spirit Guides," and "Use Your Psychic Calendar."

Clairaudience

Do you ever just know what song is going to come up in your playlist shuffle next? Or "hear" the phone ring before it actually rings? Clairaudience is "clear hearing"; this is your ability to "hear" messages from Spirit and your Higher Self, either with your actual physical ears or within your own mind's voice. It can also be a voice that is in your mind, but it is not your own. With practice, you will be able to distinguish between the many voices within yourself, from your own thoughts to spirit messages. In Part 2, you will practice clairaudience in activities including "Read a Picture's Energy," "Practice Remote Viewing," and "Send a Telepathic Text."

Clairsentience

Have you ever been compelled to ask a stranger how they were doing, simply because you felt they were sad or feeling out of place? Do you feel inexplicable joy when someone accomplishes something, even if you don't know them very well? Clairsentience is "clear feeling"; this is your ability to feel emotions that are connected to someone else. Just as Spirit uses your five physical senses to deliver messages, your emotions are also used for this purpose. You may be able to see behind the masks that others wear. You may know what is going on even when they insist that "Everything is fine!" You can feel the truth as strongly as your own emotions. Picking up on others' emotions as a conduit and also receiving an emotion as a signal of what is happening are both spiritual gifts that your guides, loved ones on the other side, and Higher Self want you to pay more attention to.

Clairsentience can also manifest physically. For example, you may feel nauseous or sick when something dubious is about to happen to you or to someone else, or you may have a "shadow pain" when you are picking up on another's health issues. Shadow pain is a sympathy pain, or a pain you mirror in yourself to communicate a pain you feel in someone else. It's not as intense as the actual pain, but it gives a message nonetheless.

As you develop your psychic skills, you will be able to differentiate between your own emotions and the ones you feel from others. In Part 2, clairsentience is incorporated into many activities, including "Sense Someone Else's Feelings," "Receive Messages from Objects," and "Receive Messages from Ancestral Photos."

Claircognizance

Has there been a time when you knew someone had terrible intentions, even though you didn't personally know that person? Have you ever had a name pop into your head when speaking to someone, and when mentioning it, it was relevant to that person's life in some way? Claircognizance is "clear knowing"; this is your ability to simply know something without having any empirical evidence to back it up. This psychic knowledge can feel very factual and is usually not as apparent to others as it is to you. As you practice your psychic abilities, you'll learn how to differentiate this understanding from a simple hunch or something that you want to happen. In Part 2, you will have the opportunity to practice your claircognizance in activities such as "Test Your Long-Term Psychic Predictions," "Perform a House Cleansing and Blessing," and "Choose a Crystal for Psychic Work."

Clairalience

When sitting in a room, have you ever suddenly smelled a floral scent from seemingly nowhere? Or, when going about your day, have you smelled a dish your late grandmother used to cook? Clairalience is "clear smelling"; this is your ability to smell something that is not in your physical environment. Oftentimes, this ability is linked to spirit messages from either spirit guides or loved ones on the other side reaching out. Clairalience is a gift that may surprise you, as it can pop up unexpectedly in many activities in Part 2. Be extra mindful to focus on your clear smelling in the activity "Communicate with Pets," as it's often a favorite way they send you messages!

Clairgustance

Do you ever experience random tastes in your mouth for no apparent reason? Do they come with strong pulls, perhaps a drive to remember something or deliver a message to someone? Clairgustance is "clear tasting"; this is your ability to taste something without actual food or substance. Over time, you'll realize that this is another way to receive energetic messages that deliver insight and assistance to those they are intended for. In Part 2, you may find yourself surprised to experience clairgustance in a variety of activities. The activity "Receive Messages from Ancestral Photos" may bring this psychic skill more into focus.

TAPPING INTO INTUITION

There is a voice deep within you—one that is not just yours. It's the shared voice of ancient wisdom and a link to the collective consciousness. It's a whisper from the universe that is always available to you. It is your intuition, and as you learned previously, it is a piece of your psychic abilities.

Tapping into this voice will make you stronger as a psychic, and you will grow in confidence through using it. This is where your psychic journey truly begins. The following are key things to keep in mind as you use and strengthen your intuition, both in this book and beyond.

The Key Is You

Becoming psychic is actually about becoming *you*. You are about to learn more about yourself than ever before, and in doing so, learn to decipher messages from beyond. As you launch yourself onto this path, remember that you are traveling *inward*. All the answers are within you. As you wake these insights up from their dormant states, you will find yourself awakening in ways you never dreamed possible. Becoming psychic is a healing journey; it's one where you can release wounds of the past and relinquish their hold on how you operate today and in the future.

You cannot tap into your intuition and develop your psychic skills without shedding the layers that are not serving you. You will naturally notice what these layers are as you encounter the obstacles that come with becoming psychic. For example, using your voice might be difficult if you are always one to worry about what others think. You may start to notice how much this particular fear is holding you back in life. As you start to practice giving psychic messages to yourself and others, this fear will be faced head-on. The questions at the end of each activity in Part 2 will assist you with these obstacles and jump-start your journey to overcoming them. After each exercise, taking note of emotions, frustrations, and insights will allow you to see the things that were in your way and how to overcome them.

As you learned in the previous sections, Spirit will use you as a vessel for messages through your emotional, physical, and spiritual body. So to tap into your intuition, listen to yourself. Listen to what your sorrow is telling you. Listen to what a sudden pang in your chest is telling you. Listen to what your gut is telling you about a situation. Listening is what all successful psychics do. Like seeds planted in the ground, your intuition is planted firmly in every encounter you experience. Your psychic ability and practice will allow the seeds of intuition to sprout.

Ego versus Intuition

One of the obstacles you'll face in your psychic journey is that of the ego. The ego is the human part of yourself whose sole job is to keep you alive. The best and most effective way it does this is by trying to keep you absolutely the same. Anything that promotes change is immediately and efficiently beaten back until it no longer exists. How your ego presents itself in this particular journey is by downplaying your intuition. Self-doubt, skepticism, fear, and low self-confidence are all very powerful tools the ego uses to try to stop you from strengthening your innate abilities.

The more you understand the ego and how its function is to keep you from progressing, the better you can appreciate it but also not take it so seriously. This journey *will* change you. It will happen in little pieces along the way, but looking back, you will find yourself in a very different place in life than when you started. You may be frightened to practice your skills, to be wrong, or to tell others what you are up to! But this is a good fear: It's one that creates context for you to evolve and get closer to self and Spirit. Knowing that you are safe, surrounded by love and support, and naturally supposed to grow and change will keep that ego from being too much of a hindrance as you hone your intuition into psychic skills.

Letting Go of Judgment and Self-Doubt

The cloudiness of judgment and self-doubt, those pesky side effects of your ego, can decrease your motivation to practice your natural intuition. But practice is necessary for growth!

So to begin letting go of these obstacles presented by ego, get used to feeling doubtful and judged when leaning on your intuition. Facing that fear head-on will alleviate its effects on you. Over time, not only will you become desensitized to the ego's power, but you will also take away all its control.

Receiving validation from open-minded friends, from your own record keeping, and from Spirit will help keep your intuition strong along the way. Validation is not so that you feel correct or right; it's so you can trust what you are hearing from your intuition and become accustomed to how it feels to hear that voice. Friends who celebrate your growth and support your psychic journey will become wonderful helpers and teachers for you. Those who will allow you to practice with them and give you thoughtful and inspiring feedback to your intuitive messages are integral in your growth. Your record keeping (or journaling) will create a tangible account of your intuition. Time is another wonderful accompaniment to your skills: It will allow you to look back and see where you were correct and how it felt to get those messages. Will you make mistakes? Of course! But mistakes are the best teachers and can help you see where you let ego get in the way of your intuition.

Letting Go of Desire

Ego also brings along with it the desires that can cloud your intuition and psychic skills. For example, if you want a friend to be happy but receive a psychic message that you know will make them upset, the convenient thing would be to give them a message you *want* to give instead of the one that is true. Or you may try to ignore a gut understanding that something is not right because you don't want that to be the case. The separating of your own desires takes time, but it is an ever-present ability that you will hone through practice and mindfulness.

GETTING READY TO USE YOUR PSYCHIC ABILITIES

Tapping into the collective energy of the universe, all of its frequencies, and messengers can feel overwhelming. For this reason, there are a couple of important steps to take when preparing to psychically connect.

Step 1: Set Your Intention

The first step before any psychic exercise is to formulate your intention. Firmly stating what your intent is for performing that psychic skill will open up the path to obtaining it. Intention provides the road map to the end goal and keeps your own connection to what you want strong and steady amid the distractions of other energies, thoughts, and more.

Your intention can be to help someone, to cultivate personal growth, or simply to satisfy joyful curiosity. The desire you have is the ingredient that sets your skills ablaze. Consciously spending time to reflect on your intent helps you freshen your desire so that it works time and time again.

Your intention needs to be good in order for it to call in the highest protection and assistance from the spirit realms. You will be assisted by guides, ascended masters, and universe energy when you are setting your intention apart from your ego. Therefore, psychic practices for the purpose of helping, growing, and inspiring are going to be much more successful than anything rooted in jealousy, revenge, or malicious intent. Desire has to be highly vibrational. Because you are human, it's normal to struggle with more base desires, but part of your work will be to find the good in a psychic skill and focus on that.

So before approaching a psychic activity, have a moment of reflection with yourself. Decide what you want to do and why.

Write it down and feel clear about it. It doesn't matter how specific the intention itself is, but rather how clear you are about it to yourself. Sit with it for a few minutes, reflecting on it to ensure it's for your own highest good and the highest good of those around you.

Step 2: Perform a Centering Meditation

Meditating before a psychic practice will bring you to a comfortable vibrational level in which you will be more open to Spirit's messages; it will also strengthen the communication between you and your Higher Self. When you take this time to meditate, you are opening yourself up to the abundant knowledge and power the universe consistently provides in order to obtain the best results from your efforts. Energy will flow through you more easily, and you in turn will have a heightened ability to decipher its frequencies into messages.

Meditating can seem difficult at first because your ego will try to interfere. Understanding that fear of change, connection, and spiritual awakening can create a bit of anxiety during meditation will help you work through it. The more you meditate, the less you will find it a challenge. Eventually, you will find yourself meditating often and even multiple times throughout the day.

Where to Meditate

Over time, you will learn how and where you connect best with your own energy. However, a quiet, secluded place is always a great option so you won't be directly disturbed. This will allow you to focus on your psychic practice.

How to Meditate

Your eyes can be closed or open during meditation, though it's often recommended you close your eyes so you can focus. If you are experiencing any anxiety, it's okay to keep them open and direct your gaze to something peaceful or calm, such as a plant or a nature scene. Follow these steps to meditate:

1. Get into a comfortable position, either lying down or seated upright.
2. With eyes closed, or gently gazing upon a focal point of your choosing, take a deep breath in through your nose, hold it for three seconds, then exhale through your mouth.
3. Repeat step two a few times, envisioning a bright healing light entering you as you inhale, and any negative things releasing from you as you exhale. You may wish to softly repeat a mantra during this step. The mantras "I am whole" or "I am love" are easy ones to begin with. Anything that resonates with you is a perfect mantra that can assist in holding your focus as you meditate.
4. When you feel ready, open your eyes and end the meditation.

Check Your Ego

Thoughts and ideas will pop into your head at random as you meditate: This is your ego's attempt to get you off track. Things you forgot to do will be suddenly on your mind as you drift into a meditative state. This is the time when you suddenly remember you have to reschedule that pesky dentist's appointment, or that you forgot a key ingredient for the potato salad you are making for this weekend's big barbecue. Have a pen and paper in front of you to prepare for this to-do list your sneaky ego will provide for you. Simply write down whatever it is that comes to you, then shift your focus back to the meditation steps.

How Long to Meditate

Choose an amount of time that is doable for you and set a timer. At first, you can keep your meditation five minutes or less; however, with practice you will inherently know when to be finished. You can set your timer for an angel number that speaks to you that day, such as eleven minutes and eleven seconds, or whatever time feels right. Keep in mind that the goal is to feel a calmness, connectedness, and peace with meditation rather than to sit quietly for a specific amount of time.

Meditation Script

The following is a script you can use to meditate before any psychic activity. You can read it through to get familiar with it first, and then self-talk your way through it before your psychic activity, or you may want to record it on a device to easily play whenever you are ready to meditate.

> *"Let's begin the meditation. Lie or sit comfortably and close your eyes if desired. Inhale through your nose for three seconds, hold it for three seconds, then exhale through your mouth for three seconds. Again, inhale, and feel your entire body tense up. Now open your mouth and release the air completely from your lungs. One more time: Inhale, hold, and exhale.*
>
> *With breathing happening in a more natural and effortless flow, you may now envision your intention for this exercise. Feel it descend upon you, a bright white light that enters you through your heart chakra. As it enters, you feel a warmth spreading throughout you. Let it absorb through you. Let it settle into every cell, every muscle, and every bone. You feel it sewn into your soul.*
>
> *Take a deep breath in through your nose now, and with it, take in this power you feel. Hold it for three seconds, really feeling its goodness disperse through your entire self, and*

then release the breath through your mouth, knowing that your intention has set and solidified, becoming part of your energy. Now, feel a wave of gratitude for Spirit's interaction and assistance sweep over you. It's a little wave at first, and as it moves through you, it washes over you with power. Inhale the gratitude through your nose for three seconds. Hold it for three seconds. Release anything residual you intuitively know you no longer need through your mouth. Allow yourself now to feel thankful for the assistance you are going to be provided from Spirit. Feel grateful the universe has given you the tools to work toward this intention.

Sit in this feeling, however it expresses itself now. When you are ready, open your eyes."

With this script on hand, you are now prepared to take the next step in your psychic journey: completing the activities in the following pages of this book!

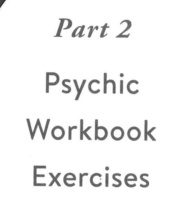

Part 2

Psychic
Workbook
Exercises

As you discover your psychic abilities, you will discover yourself. Meeting your authentic self is the gift of being psychic, for your talents lie within you. They are embedded in your intuition, emotions, spirituality, physical senses, and more. For this reason, you will notice a common thread in the following activities: you. Each activity guides you in becoming closer to your emotional, spiritual, or physical self as you develop a specific psychic practice. The nuances of who you are will help you unlock the secrets of the energies around you during these activities. Becoming psychic can also increase your confidence and self-love, as you uncover just how multifaceted and capable you are.

You may find yourself attracted to some activities more than others. While it's important to try everything to see which exercises you connect to more than others, don't feel you need to connect to all aspects of the psychic realm. Every activity you devote time to will awaken a part of you that has perhaps lain dormant for years or has whispered feverishly for you to notice it. You will find that the more you try, the more you will be capable of. Practice is important, as many of these gifts take time and effort to get a firm grasp on. Approach these activities with an open mind and a joyful heart. You are about to enter a path that can bring you profound peace and insight. You are ready for this journey simply because you already are psychic. You'll find that what may currently seem normal to you is sometimes a very special psychic gift.

1 Open Your Third Eye

Have you ever wondered at the ability of children to "see" more than adults can? The baby who smiles and laughs at seemingly nothing, or the child who can create a rocket ship out of a cardboard box? Children are adept at engaging their third eye (the part of you that can see beyond the physical realm) as a form of play or creativity, and it often integrates with their imagination. But the third eye gets dimmed as we age. Society compels us to be more practical and in line with what our physical eyes can see.

However, to really awaken psychic gifts, opening the third eye is an essential part of your practice. This fundamental tool will be used in every psychic activity you do—both in this book and beyond—and will surprise you with its utility even when you aren't asking it to work!

Seeing from your third eye is different from seeing with your imagination or thoughts. Learning the distinction is part of the practice. The third eye sees beyond this world and is able to see the true world: the unified connection between Spirit and the physical plane. When you see from your third eye, it will feel organic and new. You may see colors brightly. You may see faces of people you do not know and visions of worlds you've never been to before. It's not linked to knowledge you know you have, and it feels as if you are "looking" at something new and for the first time. Just as if you went out in the world and saw things with your eyes, these visions will be presented to you, not created by you. Over time, you'll come to know this difference for yourself.

GETTING READY

Opening the third eye takes effort. It's possibly quite groggy from being closed for many years, so having patience is important. To prepare, start seeing beyond what this world shows you in your day-to-day activities. The third eye is activated by using it with intention. Paying more mindful attention to the beauty you see with your physical eyes and feeling filled with wonder by it is what assists your third eye to awaken within you. Incorporating this third eye activation through mindful awareness to the details around you should be a daily, constant activity. The timeline for your own progress will be different from anyone else's. Focus on your own enjoyment and insight, and it will go at a pace that is right for you.

Once you have practiced this for a while, you will be ready for the following more guided activity to truly open your third eye. Begin this activity in a quiet spot. Do your meditation practice included in Part 1 and, while meditating, specifically focus on the area between your eyebrows, as this is where the third eye is located. You may want to do this while lying or sitting, or even before bedtime. You may want to tap your finger on your third eye, or just lightly press and hold your finger on it. You may wish to place a favorite crystal on your third eye in order to amplify your focus (see the "Choose a Crystal for Psychic Work" activity).

How to Open Your Third Eye

1. Once ready, send gratitude to the space you are inhabiting and ask Spirit to give you a vision.
2. As you begin to see something, really focus your attention there. It could be a swirl of colors, a face, or even flashes of moving pictures and events you don't understand. Don't try to control this vision; just observe. Asking yourself what you are

seeing and noticing details are good ways to remain separate from the vision and avoid trying to control it.

3. When you start feeling distracted, it's time for the activity to end. You will notice you will be able to do this activity for longer durations as you continue to practice.

4. Take notes about what you saw, either by writing or drawing.

Check Your Senses

As you explore the visions of your third eye, question what you are seeing and feeling throughout the exercise: This helps you observe what you experience and keeps you from being drawn into the vision—or from nodding off. If you feel yourself slipping into day-dreams, stop the exercise for now. The point is to simply see what your third eye is showing you, not create visions yourself.

As you get better at using your third eye, it will stay open all the time. You may find yourself in the presence of someone and suddenly see their aura glow around them or see a loved one standing beside them. There are so many ways the third eye will operate during your psychic journey.

TRY IT OUT

Follow the steps described to open your third eye. Record your answers to these questions to reflect on your experience:

+ What vision did I see at first?
+ What colors or symbols did I see?
+ How did I feel when I was in this state? Emotionally? Physically?
+ How do I know this was a vision and not my imagination?
+ How did this "seeing" feel different from imagining things?

2 Perform an Energy Scan of Your Environment

Any space you walk into has a particular energetic vibration that you will pick up on. It could be a positive energy, like at a party or celebration, or a more negative one, like if someone's just been arguing and the room feels tense. The energies you encounter from a place can feel overwhelming if you aren't sure how to manage them—do you welcome them or protect yourself from them? Becoming aware of the type of energy around you will help you strengthen your psychic connections.

You have a natural ability to "read a room"—namely, using your intuition. The first and most important lesson with energy scans is that you are not making this up! You were made to do this but taught to ignore it. Society says that without concrete proof in your physical world, the things you feel and pick up on cannot be trusted. And while tangible evidence is important to take into consideration, strengthening your intuition will create the logic within that can be just as beneficial to you as "concrete proof" from the physical world. Every space has energy. Taking the time to sit with it will allow you to know what that energy is and what you can do with it.

GETTING READY

Sit in a room, preferably in a public setting. This can be a library or coffee shop. It's best if it's a place you can sit and comfortably observe everyone around you. You can do this anywhere, but stores with aisles and tall cupboards make it harder for energy to flow consistently. You will want to be in a section of the room that intuitively feels neutral to you (and also be out of the way).

Set yourself up with a journal and pen in this spot. Enter a calm, meditative state using the meditation exercise provided in Part 1 as you take a moment to clear your mind and energy.

How to Perform an Energy Scan

1. Start to scan the room from your seat. Allow your attention to lead you. See where it turns first.
2. Make notes of what immediate feelings you have without questioning yourself. You may feel curious about a section or even a person.
3. You can start to focus on someone when you feel curious. This is not an accident! Now is the time to ask yourself why you feel attracted to this energy and what it actually feels like. Nervousness or curiosity, anxiousness or excitement are all emotions that may bubble to the surface. Diving deeper will make sense of what they signify. Creating an empathic connection is essential here because many times you are feeling the feelings of others. Emotions are conduits for Spirit. Feelings like curiosity, avoidance, stress, insecurity, or interest are actually you picking up on the vibrations not only of other people, but of the space itself. It's very normal to start to feel compelled to reach out to someone you are seeing in the room. As you get better at scanning an environment, you'll see that you are getting messages from others' energies. Don't be surprised if someone comes up to you and is curious about you too. Being open like this in a public setting will alert some of the more intuitive people around you to come and say "hello" even if they don't know why they are doing it! (Some of us naturally interact energetically like this in our environment all the time. Are you the type

of person who strangers tend to seek out in grocery stores or other public places? It's possible you've been energetically interacting with strangers your entire life without realizing it.)

4. Continue to jot down as many notes as you can about the room about you. If you are inclined to draw, this is also a tool you can utilize to sketch where in the room the energy feels bottled up or flows. You can even section off the map to highlight where energy feels stagnant, flexible, positive, or negative.

Check Your Ego
There is a difference between judging others and feeling their vibrations. Thinking about whether you like someone's outfit or the design of a room is not an energy scan in the way that is outlined here. This practice is not people watching; it's energy scanning. Being watchful of your mindset and keeping it on track will help you strengthen this psychic skill.

TRY IT OUT

Follow the steps described to perform an energy scan of your environment. Record your answers to these questions to reflect on your experience:

+ What did it feel like to be attracted to one area of the room more than another?
+ Was I pulled more by negative feelings or positive ones?
+ What was I curious about? What did that feel like?
+ Where did my ego mindset come in to try to interfere? How does that feel different from picking up energy?
+ What symbols, images, letters, or names did I intuitively pick up on?
+ How did I feel before the scan? After?

3 Sense Someone Else's Feelings

One of the most common ways your psychic gift will manifest and gain strength is through the channel of your own emotions. Everything around you is energy, and your emotions are conduits of its highs, lows, and subtle nuances. Many times throughout your life you've probably felt emotions that were not yours but have most likely shrugged them off or ignored them completely. Getting in the habit of acknowledging and examining these moments is how you will find access to a plethora of psychic messages.

As you learned in Part 1, clairsentience is the ability of "clear feeling." It can manifest in your ability to experience others' feelings and traumas. When you become an emotional conduit, you begin to not only understand that the emotions you are feeling are not always yours; you also become self-aware enough to identify where and why the emotions are coming to you. You could experience these emotions as you connect to a living person or one who has crossed over. You could also pick up emotional energies in spaces and events.

A fundamental skill you will learn is to differentiate the feelings of others from your own and to subsequently choose your response to these messages. Most likely you have already been feeling energies that are not yours regularly, so it's not so much about learning how to do it; rather, it's about noticing and separating the sources of energetic input.

GETTING READY

Scanning your own emotions for messages is a fundamental step in preparing to be an emotional conduit. (It is also part of a number of other psychic practices in this book.) This scan includes checking how you feel emotionally, your five physical senses, and also your physical and emotional feelings of stress or elation. The purpose is to establish a baseline of your own default emotional and physical states before tapping into another's energy.

To get in the habit of scanning your emotions regularly, you are going to create a "three-word journal" in your calendar, a specific notebook, smartphone notes app, or other chosen method of recording. You will be writing down your feelings three words at a time, three times a day. You may pair this activity with mealtimes or whenever you already have an existing schedule to make it an easier habit to create.

Once you've decided where and when you will write your feelings and set up your method for remembering to do this activity, take a moment to enter a calm and meditative state. Use the meditation guide in Part 1 or your own preferred practice.

How to Become an Emotional Conduit

1. At the decided times during the day, ask yourself, "How do I feel?" and write down three words that describe your immediate feelings. You do not have to write sentences or elaborate further. At first, the entries may be very simple and the feelings you generate may be very basic. In the beginning, adjectives such as "hungry," "tired," or "anxious" will suffice. Later on, feelings will become more articulate, such as "vulnerable," "introspective," or "optimistic." If you find yourself struggling to come up with feelings at all, this is an amazing indicator of how much self-connection you may be missing out on throughout the day. Be patient with yourself! It's okay to find this activity

challenging. Over time, it will become not only second nature but also highly therapeutic.

2. As you go about your day after writing your three words, ask yourself why you feel this way. If you wrote down "anxious," for example, ponder what the context surrounding that anxiety is. Perhaps it's an email from a coworker? Or an uncomfortable interaction you had with a store clerk? The point is to see where this feeling originated and if it's truly yours or a reaction to someone else you've had contact with in some way. You can record these reasons in your three-word journal beside your recorded emotions. Being able to link your emotions with their sources can unlock countless patterns in your day and even your whole life.

Over time, you will see your entries getting deeper, more profound, and more specific. You will be better able to identify exactly how you feel and whether you are picking it from someone else or it is really your own feeling. You will be able to automatically sense when an energy you are carrying in the form of an emotion or feeling is not yours. The subtle nuances will grow to be obvious.

TRY IT OUT

Follow the steps described for at least three days to become an emotional conduit. Record your answers to these questions to reflect on your experience:

+ What are your three words right now?
+ Is it difficult to answer the question "How do I feel?" Why or why not?
+ Choose one feeling and reflect upon it. Where does it come from?
+ What do you notice about your entries as they have progressed over time?
+ How has this activity evolved for you as you've practiced it?

4 Create a Protection Bubble

There are energies around you all the time. These energies come from people, places, and events. They want to communicate with you in various ways, oftentimes clinging to your emotions or physical body, and at times your inner thoughts, in order to do it. Many people allow them in due to not knowing what they are or how to stop them. This can create feelings of overwhelm, anxiety, sadness, and sometimes even a numb detachment. Being self-aware of your own energy in response to the energies that attempt to infiltrate will be a fundamental part of your psychic skill set. Creating a protection bubble will help you stay in control of your own energy and decide which other energies you let in. It keeps you in touch with energies around you while maintaining your spiritual sovereignty.

Opening yourself up to the energy of Spirit has both blessings and challenges. You will find yourself becoming automatically more attuned to others' feelings, their base issues that they themselves may not be aware of, and messages from those on the other side. You will feel others' intentions toward you and the world. You will get random messages and visions you know nothing about. It's a by-product of connection, and while it can at times be staggering, it is also a lovely gift.

GETTING READY

Once you learn how to create a protection bubble, you will find that it becomes more natural and easier to produce over time. After grasping the concept and giving it a few tries, you'll be able to snap it up around you in mere seconds in any situation or environment. Wayward energies from people and environments will always try to poke their way in, but this stops them immediately. Knowing the purpose of this bubble is the first step in creating it. It keeps the communication from Spirit polite and respectful. You'll find it a lovely method to feel like yourself and in control of any psychic practice situation.

Prepare to create your bubble by finding a quiet space to be alone. Make sure you will not be disturbed, and that you feel completely comfortable, so you will be better able to be vulnerable and calm throughout.

How to Create Your Protection Bubble

1. Lying or sitting with your eyes closed, take several deep breaths in and out.

2. Starting at the crown of your head, envision a light shining down upon you. Knowing that this light is from the divine, most infinite source of love and light, allow it to enter your crown chakra on the top of your head.

3. Very slowly and with intention, envision the light traveling throughout each part of your body, from the tips of your ears to your toes. Every inch of you is saturated with this light.

4. Take a few breaths as you feel this light filling you, healing you, shining on all the parts of you that can feel unseen and unheard. You may feel loved, calm, peaceful, and sometimes even emotional. If you fall asleep, you'll have to try this again! But being tired is a good indication it's working to relax you.

5. Now, imagine all this light and imagine it's extending out from you 6 to 8 inches in all directions. Envision it releasing and creating a bubble of light around you, back and front, top and bottom.

6. See yourself floating in a bubble of beautiful, brilliant light. Do you see a color in this bubble? That's your aura! (Your aura is

your energy signature. It's the part of your energy that is inherently you and no one else.) This bubble of light has a clear shell around it; you'll be able to "see" through it with your third eye. Even though it's transparent, it's a strong barrier, effectively stopping any outside energies you don't want from coming in. You don't have to know how it does this; your Higher Self and divine intuition are working all the time to create the right balance here.

7. When you feel like you can disengage from this practice, simply take a few breaths and return to the room you are in with open eyes and a peaceful state of mind.

8. Lying or sitting where you are for a moment, note the good work you just did. This light is never going away. Even when your third eye is not seeing it, you can rest assured it is around you all the time. It's your protection bubble, and you can call upon it at any time to protect you and secure your defenses against outside, unwanted influences.

TRY IT OUT

Follow the steps described to form your protection bubble. Record your answers to these questions to reflect on your experience:

+ How did I feel in this bubble of light?
+ Did I find it hard or easy to create it?
+ What visions, if any, did I experience that surprised me?
+ What colors did I see?
+ How did I feel afterward?

5 Balance Your Chakras

Feeling off balance, disconnected, and numb at times is a part of life. And these emotions impact your energy. There are seven points of energy in your body known as the chakras. Chakra means "wheel" in Sanskrit, and the chakras are believed to be spinning disks of energy aligned throughout your body to maintain emotional, spiritual, and physical well-being (when they are flowing without difficulty).

When a chakra is "blocked," or not flowing properly, it can diminish the qualities associated with that part of your energetic body. When a chakra is overactive, it can intensify those corresponding qualities to the point of overwhelm. Keeping your energy flowing through each chakra in a balanced way creates a healthy connection between self and Spirit. It can restore you when you feel fatigued and cue you into what isn't flowing so you can take the time and care to heal yourself.

The following are the names, locations, associated colors, and meanings for each chakra:

1. **Root Chakra.**
   Location: Base of the spine. Color: Red. Meaning: Grounding, stability, identity.
   When this chakra is blocked, you can feel insecure in your life. Overall safety and well-being feel jeopardized. An overactive root chakra can result in aggressive and hyperactive behaviors. When the root chakra is in alignment, you feel a sense of security, personal power and identity, and emotional peace within.

2. **Sacral Chakra.**
   Location: Just below the belly button. Color: Orange. Meaning: Creativity, joy, sexuality.
   When this chakra is blocked, there can be feelings of worthlessness and a loss of personal value. An overactive sacral chakra can result in arrogant and controlling behavior. When the sacral chakra is in alignment, there is a joyful sensuality that connects you to others and yourself, as well as a healthy self-worth.

3. **Solar Plexus Chakra.**
   Location: Upper stomach area. Color: Yellow. Meaning: Confidence and self-esteem.
   When this chakra is blocked, there is a lack of self-belief and a stagnancy in new projects and opportunities. An overactive solar plexus chakra can result in overly critical and judgmental behaviors. When the solar plexus chakra is in alignment, you have a strong self-belief and feel motivated to try new things.

4. **Heart Chakra.**
   Location: Center of the chest. Color: Green. Meaning: Love.
   When this chakra is blocked, you are putting yourself last, never receiving the love you need. An overactive heart chakra can result in jealous or angry outbursts. When the heart chakra is in alignment, there is an increase in the ability to receive love and see the worth in yourself and everyone around you.

5. **Throat Chakra.**
   Location: Throat. Color: Blue. Meaning: Communication.
   When this chakra is blocked, you experience many issues with self-expression and self-advocacy. An overactive throat chakra can result in low self-awareness, including overtaking conversations and interrupting others. When the throat chakra is in alignment, there is a healthy expression of self, presented with confidence, compassion, and appropriate assertiveness.

6. **Third Eye Chakra.**
   Location: Between the eyes on the bridge of your nose. Color: Indigo. Meaning: Intuition, visualization, sight.

When this chakra is blocked, you can become easily misled by others, false opportunities, and roads pointing you to self-destruction. An overactive third eye chakra can create a lack of control when making choices, as well as a feeling of impatience. When the third eye chakra is in alignment, there is a strong and confident connection to your natural intuition and the ability to see beyond what this earth plane allows. (Also see the "Open Your Third Eye" activity.)

7. **Crown Chakra.**
   Location: Top of the head. Color: Violet or white. Meaning: Connection.

   When this chakra is blocked, there is an overall nature of stagnancy, stubbornness, and skepticism. When the crown chakra is in alignment, it creates a pure connection to your spiritual gifts and overall purpose in this lifetime. This chakra is used to keep all the other chakras open, and therefore brings a state of enlightenment and peace when balanced.

GETTING READY

Once you have an understanding of the seven chakras, you are on the path to balancing them! Before beginning this chakra-balancing meditation, find a quiet space to practice and use your chosen method to get into a meditative state.

How to Balance Your Chakras

1. Close your eyes. Take deep breaths in through your nose and out through your mouth until you feel comfortable and secure.
2. Begin with your root chakra at the base of your spine. Envision a red glow emanating from and surrounding this location. Think about what this chakra does and know that your infinite wisdom will give it what it needs to rebalance and stabilize. See its glow burn brighter.

3. Allow your awareness to move up to your belly button to your sacral chakra. Repeat step two.
4. Continue repeating step two with each remaining chakra in this order: solar plexus chakra, heart chakra, throat chakra, third eye chakra, crown chakra.

TRY IT OUT

Follow the steps described to balance your chakras. Record your answers to these questions to reflect on your experience:

+ Was it difficult to envision and connect with my chakras? Why or why not?
+ Did my energy feel stuck anywhere specific during this activity? Where?
+ Why did this chakra feel blocked?
+ What did it feel like to unblock this chakra?
+ What emotions did I experience during this activity?
+ How do I feel now that I have completed this balancing practice?

6 Connect with the Earth

You're probably well aware that being outside in nature lifts your mood. The vibrations of nature are perfectly in tune and run through everything—every tree and plant, every season, every animal. When you purposely align with these vibrations and recognize your inner power, your emotional, spiritual, and physical bodies become healthier and more receptive to spirit messages.

Grounding (mindfully connecting to nature) is a simple way to align yourself with nature, and it is available to you at any time, in any season.

GETTING READY

Grounding is a habit that takes practice to truly establish and do effectively. For this reason, it's best to create a foundational grounding practice first. Begin by preparing your morning routine for grounding work. Think ahead at nighttime so that you set yourself up for morning success: Place your phone far away from your bed to limit the urge to reach for it when you awaken, go to bed at a good time so that you will get enough hours of sleep to feel fully rested in the morning, and avoid using technology right before you try to fall asleep.

In the morning, pour yourself a large glass of water and drink it outside in the sunlight. If it's too cold to do this outdoors or the weather isn't favorable, sit by a well-lit window to drink. Take your time drinking your water (fifteen minutes is recommended) and simply being present. Be mindful of the nature around you (or the nature beyond your window). This is a wonderful time to meditate, balance your chakras, or do any other spiritual practice you enjoy.

In addition to practicing this foundational grounding exercise, get used to going out in all kinds of weather. Rainy, windy, snowy, and foggy days are all beautiful in their own unique ways. Learning to embrace nature exactly the way it presents itself to you is important. Nature is a teacher of adaptability and evolution. It shows us how change is a beautiful transition, not something to be fearful of. Notice how your flexibility over time will allow you to find the beauty in all weather days. Think about how this relates to seeing beauty in all parts of life, even the less "sunny" moments.

How to Ground Yourself

Once you've established a bit of a routine with mindfully experiencing nature every morning, you can level up this grounding practice to reach higher realms of connection. The following are simple ways to do so. Try not to take on too much at once. You can change things daily depending on what you know you intuitively need from nature.

✦ **Barefoot walking.** Take your shoes off and walk along a path or in an open area. With each step, focus on how the earth feels on your feet. Take time to be curious about the world around you. See all the beauty that hides in plain sight. Touch trees, flowers, or rocks as you go. If you need a rest, sit on the ground.

✦ **Meditate outside.** Take out your yoga mat or favorite lawn chair and perform your daily meditation outdoors. Sitting in the morning light or comfortable shade, appreciate the smells, sights, and sounds that accompany your mindful meditation. Ask yourself what you hear, see, and smell. Savor the beauty of nature and allow wonder to saturate your being. Make a mental list of what you are grateful for in your life as you meditate.

- **Create art in nature.** Are there things you see outside that inspire you? Take your journal into nature and write poems or uplifting thoughts about the world you are looking at. Or perhaps you wish to draw or find hidden gems to photograph. With your artist's eye, you can see so much.
- **Study nature.** Have you always had an affinity for research and learning more about our world? That is a form of grounding. Grow a garden or take up bird-watching. Start tracking the daily weather or make some notes about what flora and fauna call your backyard home. Follow a curiosity and see where it leads you.

Notice the thoughts that come to you during your grounding sessions. You are likely to experience "spiritual downloads," which are intense, life-changing truths that come suddenly from seemingly out of nowhere, but that are actually arriving to you from Spirit.

TRY IT OUT

Follow the steps described to practice grounding. Record your answers to these questions to reflect on your experience:

- What do I find difficult or distracting about grounding?
- What helps me to create a consistent grounding practice?
- What grounding activities are most rewarding to me? Why?
- When I start my day with a grounding practice, how do I feel afterward?
- What revelations have been given to me during grounding sessions?

7 Interpret Your Dreams

Dreams are a source of valuable insight. This is a time in your routine when the ego is put to rest, and the deep recesses of your subconscious can shine through to you, offering important introspection. Think of your dreams as a gateway to all the things you are holding on to. The more you start to pay attention to what you dream about, the more you will create connections between you, Spirit, and your Higher Self.

GETTING READY

At first, it can be difficult to even remember your dreams. You wake up, and immediately your ego wants to wipe away all memories of sleep and focus on the tangible world around you. But you can counteract this by writing your dreams down as soon as you wake up. Place a journal and pen beside your bed. If you care about what page you are going to be writing on, make sure it's open to that page before you go to sleep so that you don't waste precious seconds trying to find the right place for your notes when you wake up. The key here is to make it as easy as you can to go from dreaming to writing. Every waking moment, you lose more of your connection to that dream state—and the important information it holds. The solution is to create flow with the proactive placement of supplies!

It is also helpful to have some upfront knowledge of the different types of dreams you will experience. There are three types: dreams of your subconscious, visitations from loved ones on the other side, and visitations with spirit guides.

Dreams of your subconscious are helpful in understanding what in your psyche is holding you back. These are usually the dreams that feel terrifying or ridiculous. Many symbols can emerge in these types of dreams. Common themes like being naked in public or experiencing panic while all your teeth fall out represent deeply embedded insecurities and stress over important life changes. They remind you of all the things you are distracting yourself from but need to deal with.

While you sleep, it's also easier for loved ones who have crossed over to make contact with you. These dreams will often be accompanied by strong emotions. They can stay with you long after you wake up, as you often will feel that the events of the dream actually happened. You can see your loved one. They may speak to you or deliver messages nonverbally. You can simply just "know" what they want to tell you. These are often very comforting, albeit emotional, experiences and are a gift of Spirit.

Dreaming of your spirit guides is going to be increasingly common the more you work with your psychic gifts. Spirit guides are ready to help you hone your natural ability to tune in to other planes. When you sleep, it can be a particularly busy time for your spirit guides. They will talk to you, visit you, and deliver important messages for your spiritual growth.

Beyond these primary dream types, there are also countless themes that come up often for people and are linked to certain meanings. You can find exhaustive lists of themes and their meanings online or in dream interpretation books.

How to Interpret Your Dreams

1. Set an intention for dreaming before going to sleep. Tell your Higher Self that you will be accepting messages from dreams tonight and that you wish to remember all that you can about your dreams once you wake up. You may want to explore different options for recording your dreams. Writing in a journal is

advantageous because you will find yourself wanting to flip back to discover patterns, common themes, and messages. You may also wish to use an audio recording app, especially if you find it easier to talk than write. You can transcribe what you've said later into a journal for deeper reflection.

2. Go to sleep as you normally would. As soon as you wake up, start writing. What you write isn't as important as getting the details down. Create lists with emotions, symbols, and places. Ignore grammar and get it down on the page. Feverishly write all you can remember.

3. Later, once you're more awake, review those details as you reflect on what your dream(s) meant. You can use the information provided about types of dreams and common symbols and also look online for more guidance in interpreting specific dream elements.

Keep in mind that your dreams are about you. Although there are many resources that can help you in your understanding, you will always be the best one to decipher the true meanings and messages of your own dreams.

TRY IT OUT

Follow the steps described to interpret your dreams. Record your answers to these questions to reflect on your experience:

+ What types of dreams do I have the most?
+ What dreams do I love?
+ What dreams do I hate?
+ What is one dream that is repetitive for me? What could it mean?

8 Meet One of Your Spirit Guides

As you learned in Part 1 of this book, the high-vibrational beings that surround you always and dedicate themselves to your growth and spiritual evolution are called spirit guides. Some people refer to them as angels or ascended masters. No matter what you choose to call them, their purpose is the same: to guide you, assist you, and get you back on track when you have strayed from your soul's path. Everyone comes to this earth plane with a to-do list of sorts. Your Higher Self has goals and levels it wants you to reach and attain. When you are aligning with your to-do list, you feel happy, at peace, and high vibrational. Nevertheless, the distractions of physical reality are never-ending. Spirit guides can only do so much to direct and inspire you in your goals without your contribution; they need you to reach out and ask for their assistance.

Your spirit guides are an integral part of your journey to strengthen your psychic abilities. They will be finding many ways to contact you and get you to pay attention to how you can obtain all you want! A formal introduction can be helpful to get the ball rolling and make space for your spirit guides on the journey.

Meeting your spirit guides won't be the first time you've actually "met" them. They've been around you since before you were even "you" in this lifetime. They know you well and love you unconditionally. Acquainting yourself with them in an intentional way allows you to feel the support and guidance they so willingly want to offer.

GETTING READY

Because you are already walking in the energy of your spirit guides by tapping into your psychic abilities, your spirit guides are close by and eager to chat. Meditations (such as the one provided here) can help you see and interact with your guides. To prepare, use the script in Part 1—or your preferred practice—to get into a calm, meditative state. This should be done in a quiet place away from technology and distraction. Nature is a lovely spot for this activity. The "Open Your Third Eye" activity is a good precursor to this exercise. Try it out if you haven't already.

How to Meet One of Your Spirit Guides

1. Sit or lie down (with your eyes closed if possible) in your chosen spot. Take several deep, cleansing breaths.
2. Using your third eye (see details on the third eye chakra in the "Open Your Third Eye" and "Balance Your Chakras" activities), visualize a solitary spot in nature. Take note of your surroundings. Ask yourself what you see, what you smell, and how you feel. Try to use all your senses to truly put yourself in this place in your third eye vision. You are taking yourself to another dimension: a neutral space for you and one of your guides to interact.
3. Now, envision a light beaming out in front of you. A figure appears within this light. The figure is hard to see at first, and however long it takes for it to fully materialize is okay. You may not see a person in their totality, just glimpses.
4. Send out a vibration of welcome and permission to come closer to you; visualize yourself holding out a hand to greet them or a light emanating from you to share with them. In this moment of contact, a connection will be made that will impart a great feeling of inspiration. Just like an introduction with a new person

in your life, a networking of sorts will occur, and because of it, exchange of information will become easier.

5. If the vision becomes faded or seems to fail, that's okay. You can try again and again. It may take some time to really see your guides. No matter how long it may take, know that they are around you continuously and will constantly send you signs, signals, numbers, and people to communicate their messages.

Regardless of whether you see them or not, ask them to send you a sign to show you their presence. Have an open mind as to what that will be.

Have Patience
Spirit guides are notoriously choosy about when and how they appear. They have a wonderful unconditional love and supportive nature about them, but they don't always do what you tell them to!

TRY IT OUT

Follow the steps described to meet one of your spirit guides. Record your answers to these questions to reflect on your experience:

✦ How did I feel going into the meditation?
✦ Where was I in my natural visualization?
✦ Did I hear anything from my guide?
✦ If contact was made, what do I feel my spirit guide's name is?
✦ Did I sense an overall message from my guide?

9 Create a Spirit Guide Symbol Book

Spirit guides are beings that are working in conjunction with your Higher Self with the goal of keeping you on your soul contract path. They work to alert you when you are off track, give you messages that can help and heal yourself and others, and create pathways of open communication between Spirit and yourself. (Revisit Part 1 for more on spirit guides and the Higher Self.)

As you begin this journey of becoming psychic, you will need new tools to communicate with your guides. After all, you are becoming more fluent in the language of Spirit. To gain further perspective and information, consider a symbol book your new dictionary! Because your spirit guides are celestial energies, they do not always communicate in words. Symbols are their more common way to get your attention and deliver messages. And because you are an individual being with unique spirit guides, you will have your own unique set of symbols. Creating a symbol book is helpful not only for deciphering future messages but also for strengthening the meaning of each symbol given to you. This book will be shared by you and your spirit guides. Every time you make an entry, you are sealing the meaning for all time.

GETTING READY

Get a journal large enough to be used for many years. This is an ongoing manifesto of work that will take a long time to create and will never be quite completed. To prepare for creating your book, you must identify symbols that are meaningful to you. Perhaps you've always seen certain symbols such as feathers, dimes, or particular animals. So as to not overwhelm yourself, create a list of things you feel connected to symbolically. They all will have meaning for you, even if that meaning isn't solidified just yet.

As you continue along with this journal, you will want to add new symbols to your list. Prepare for Spirit to send you many more symbols once Spirit knows you are paying attention and in a space to receive them. These symbols will come suddenly and without a lot of warning. You may see them in your third eye (see more on the third eye chakra in the "Open Your Third Eye" and "Balance Your Chakras" activities) or feel compelled to blurt out what you feel, see, or are reminded of. Perhaps during a conversation with a new friend you are suddenly compelled to remember a song you heard. You could also see a shape or even a place you've once visited. You may see random items, mythical creatures, or funny memories from your past. All these things can have meanings beyond the literal sense. For example, being reminded of a location, like New York, when you're around someone can mean they are from there or have ties there.

How to Create a Spirit Guide Symbol Book

1. Choose a symbol from your list.
2. Sit in a meditative state with your eyes open or closed. You may wish to sketch or draw the symbol in your spirit guide journal during this step.
3. Ask the question out loud—"What does this mean?"—and trust whatever answer you immediately sense.
4. If an answer doesn't seem to be coming to you right away, sit with it. Ask your guides to be more specific in showing you its meaning.

5. For the next few days, be on the lookout for how this symbol presents itself to you. Notice where you see it and when, who repeats it to you and why, and what other contexts surround it. One symbol may have many meanings. Writing them all down in your journal will help you solidify and keep track of them.

Every time you lock a symbol into your journal, your bond becomes stronger with your guides. Get in the habit of preparing to write about your symbols wherever you go. The answers regarding what these symbols signify can come on quickly and strongly, so you want to be ready to track them. Every symbol will have at least two or more meanings. You will want to leave space after each symbol entry to add additional notes as you see fit.

More Practice
The symbols will feel almost like repetitive thoughts. They can feel like little annoying reminders tugging at you. You can feel compelled to say them out loud, especially if you are seeing or feeling them around another person. Your impulses and emotions will be used by Spirit to guide your attention to symbol meanings, so be aware of this as you go along.

TRY IT OUT

Follow the steps described to create your spirit guide symbol book. Record your answers to these questions to reflect on your experience:

+ What symbols do I want to explore?
+ How do I see these symbols unfold?
+ What symbols seem to have followed me for my whole life?
+ What are unusual meanings I have noticed with my symbols?
+ What surprised me the most about this activity?

10 Practice Remote Viewing

Have you ever pictured a room perfectly without ever being in it? Or, while you were talking to a friend on the phone, did you just know they were sipping tea from a yellow mug? While we are all stationed in our own bodies, you can view the outside world energetically from within your own mind. Remote viewing is the psychic practice of exploring places with the mind by using your extrasensory perception.

Remote viewing has limitless uses and is most effective when you are specific about what you're looking for and why. You may want to utilize remote viewing for finding a lost item, animal, or person, or to see the space of someone you care about or want to connect to. You can remotely view natural resources under Earth's surface such as water, oil, or minerals. It can even be utilized to peek into closed safes or behind locked doors. It can create connections between the past and present as well, as sometimes you can "see" a place that no longer exists.

GETTING READY

This activity works best after spending time practicing the "Open Your Third Eye" activity. Once you've worked with your third eye, you will next establish where you want to remotely view and why. Connecting your desire to the practice will establish a psychic map for the energy between where you are and where you want to look.

With this practice, it's vital that you can check in on how well your remote vision lines up with the space you were attempting to see. Contact a friend who you know will be open to the idea of you remotely visiting their home, or plan to remotely view a location you can physically travel to later to affirm your visions.

You may also want to have items to help you connect to the place you are aiming to remotely view, like an object from the location, a map of the area, or a photo (the exterior of the location or some other part that is different from what you plan to view there). It's a good idea to keep a journal next to you for taking quick notes or making drawings of what you see during the vision.

How to Do Remote Viewing

1. Sit quietly, breathing in through your nose and out through your mouth a few times as you settle into your meditative space. Close your eyes.

2. Take another deep breath and focus your concentration on your third eye, the chakra between your eyebrows. Here you have limitless sight, unbound by the physical restraints of the human eye.

3. Allow your third eye sight to wander to the desired place. Use your emotions and let them lead you: Concentrate on how it feels to be there and the act of standing in that place. Do not question what you see; allow yourself to float through the scenery.

4. Pay attention to the details that you see as you spend more time there. Give yourself some time to adjust to this visualized space, as there is sometimes a period of visual confusion before centering on your planned remote viewing location.

Check Your Senses

It's time to use your five senses. You may experience flashes of imagery, connected or disconnected. You may also experience sound and smells. You may hear birds chirping or cars rushing by. You may feel a chill in the air or sense that rain is coming. You may smell something cooking. The senses are all engaged in remote viewing, and details you receive strengthen your connection to this vision.

Check Your Ego

The mind will want to judge what you are perceiving and also make assumptions. You may feel unsure at first or as though this is not going to work. You may also see a space and decide what it is based on your own creative mind rather than what details you see in the vision. Try to put these aside for now, knowing that afterward, when you physically visit the place you have remotely viewed, things that didn't make sense will.

5. When you start to feel tired, simply end your session by releasing your vision and bringing yourself back to your awareness of yourself.

6. Compare what you received during the remote viewing with the actual location. Write down what you got right and how perceiving that aspect of the space felt during the vision. Also write down what didn't exactly work and why. As you practice, you'll know which feelings to lean into and which ones to ignore or allow to pass by.

TRY IT OUT

Follow the steps described as you perform your remote viewing. Record your answers to these questions to reflect on your experience:

+ Before the session: Where do I want to remotely view and why?
+ During the session: What do I see? Feel? Notice? Touch?
+ After the session: What was "correct"? What was different?
+ After the session: Now that you are aware of the "correct" answers, what feelings came with correct observations during the vision? What feelings came with incorrect ones?

11 ◆ Look for Auras

What is your favorite color? Chances are, you just named your aura color! We all have life-force energies: colorful vibrations of energy called auras that move around us. We have a natural awareness of them, as they are able to be seen with the third eye. (See more on the third eye chakra in the "Open Your Third Eye" and "Balance Your Chakras" activities.) Auras are like an energy signature; each one is unique, and most people have a combination of two colors in their aura.

Auras aren't just for show, however. They can reveal someone's personality, how they are doing emotionally and mentally, where in their body they are feeling worn down, how they are interacting with others, and what past life traumas they may carry with them. Like personality types, auras also assist you in embracing who you are and letting go of who you think you should be. You don't have to "see" an aura with your eyes to understand it; every color of an aura has a vibration that you can pick up on and read.

GETTING READY

In order to read an aura, you first need to be in touch with how someone makes you feel emotionally and what kinds of vibrations they give off. When you meet people, stop and ask yourself which color this person reminds you of, or picture what color immediately pops out at you without any thought.

You may meet a new person and feel a bit curious and energized and see the color yellow. You could be in a conversation with a friend who is going through a difficult time and needs you to be a listening ear and see the color blue. The colors will start to merge emotions, situations, and people more and more effortlessly as you bring them into your life and use them to understand others and yourself.

Use the following aura meanings to guide you as you associate different people, feelings, and things with colors:

+ **Red:** Direct, assertive, take-charge leaders who have good natural instincts about others.
+ **Blue:** Naturally empathic and sensitive people who are compassionate and thoughtful givers.
+ **Yellow:** Organized and curious multitaskers who seek constant self-improvement and love direct, honest communication.
+ **Purple:** Creative, intuitive rebels who crave change and artistic outlets.
+ **Green:** Logical and intellectual detail-oriented thinkers who crave passionate, challenging projects that promote self-growth.
+ **Turquoise:** Compassionate, old soul, quiet healers who mirror their own selves to others.
+ **Indigo:** Absorbing empaths who have the ability to read minds and communicate nonverbally in their attempts to heal others.
+ **Pink:** Optimistic, pure, loving, innocent energies who tend to be brilliant manifestors and hopeless romantics.
+ **Orange:** Highly motivated, creative, and detail-oriented people who strive for radical and rapid change in their environments.

How to Look for Auras

1. The more familiar you become with the vibrational feelings of colors, the easier it will be to start seeing auras with your third eye. Start by taking one hand and holding it up against a white or neutral background.

2. As you stare at your hand, begin to defocus your eyes. Instead of intently staring, allow your eyes to relax. You may start to see things fuzzily or misshapenly. In this way, you are creating space for your third eye to take over.

3. Practice defocusing your eyes and strengthening your third eye vision like this for a few days to get used to the sensation. You may also extend this to the world around you, focusing on plants, pets, and even random people when you are out and about.

4. Have a friend assist you for this next part. Ask them to stand in front of a white or neutral background. Look at them and begin to defocus your eyes. As you do, what do you notice? The first thing you may see is a white glow around their body's outline. This is the first step in seeing their aura. The glow may stretch out in a hazy or wavy vibration.

5. As you practice looking at your friend with your third eye, you can see beyond this first layer to their actual aura color. (See more on the third eye chakra in the "Open Your Third Eye" and "Balance Your Chakras" activities.)

Check Your Emotions
During this exercise, ask yourself about how you feel. Does this person make you feel safe or anxious? Do they make you feel joyful, silly, spontaneous, or loved? These feelings are associated with the person's aura colors.

TRY IT OUT

Follow the steps described to look for auras. Record your answers to these questions to reflect on your experience:

Before the Practice

+ Whose aura am I reading?

During the Practice

+ How do I feel when looking at this person? Describe in detail your emotional response to their presence.
+ Does this person remind me of a color? Which one(s) and why?
+ What does the energy around them look like? Am I seeing it, or is it an impression in my mind? Describe what you see in detail.

12 Hear the World Beyond

Have you ever thought you heard something that wasn't of this world? A song playing or a voice humming to you seemingly from a distant realm? Spirit has many ways of making itself known, and one of the ways is through clairaudience. This psychic hearing ability is present in everyone, but it needs to be honed to use it to its full potential in your psychic practice. There are various ways to explore your clairaudient abilities, and everyone will have different strengths in unique areas. You may find yourself able to actually hear audible voices from the spiritual realm, like the sound of footsteps or creaking floorboards when you know you are alone. It can also materialize within your mind, different from thoughts or your own imagination. These divine sounds are loud enough within yourself to take immediate notice. They can feel foreign and from something otherworldly.

Clairaudience is an ability fostered naturally in childhood. Playing with your toys, you may have rambled on and on to yourself in a meditative state. Children don't differentiate between the voices of the "real world" and those of their clairaudient abilities. Having had an imaginary friend as a child is a strong indicator of early clairaudient abilities.

Daydreaming, talking to yourself, hearing high-pitched noises in your ear that randomly and suddenly appear, and having ideas pop into your head seemingly out of the blue are all additional cues that you are using your clairaudience. When you start asking yourself questions and leaving them open ended, Spirit will use clairaudience to answer. The purpose of the messages is to bring guidance when needed and help you connect to the other side.

It is important to note that clairaudience is a joyful habit of mind, not one that induces anxiety or is a symptom of a diagnosed condition. These voices and moments of hearing the other side should never bring you distress in any way. If this is causing you stress and interfering in your relationships, it's important to see a medical professional to discuss.

GETTING READY

Learning how to listen and isolate sounds will strengthen your overall clairaudient abilities. The confusing part of this ability is that you may not recognize the difference between your actual and psychic hearing. If you have been none the wiser your entire life, it may surprise you how clairaudient you already are. Do songs get stuck in your head so well that you actually "hear" all the instruments and the tone of the singer's voice? Do you "hear" memories in your head of when someone said something to you? Can you hear the phone ring a moment before it does or feel what song is about to come on before a single note is played? Time to learn what else you can do!

To prepare, you will want to find a quiet spot in nature where you won't be bothered. Sit comfortably with your eyes closed.

How to Practice Clairaudience

1. In your spot outside, begin to simply listen. Hear birds sing, cars whoosh past, a child's laughter, the wind rustling leaves. It's amazing the sounds you will hear that you are accustomed to ignoring.
2. Then, choose a sound and attempt to isolate it. Fixate your hearing only on that sound, feeling its vibrations and getting curious about how it moves, flows, and vibrates around you.
3. After cementing this sound in your mind, return to your daily activities.

4. Before going to sleep that night, lie in bed and remember the sound you focused on in nature. Re-create it beat for beat in your head. Hear it as if it's happening right now. The familiar way you connected with it earlier in the day will guide you through this sound re-creation process now.

5. Once you have re-created the sound, you are ready for sleep.

Over time, this activity will become so easy that you will be able to understand what you are hearing versus what you are psychically hearing. When you can do this better, Spirit will give you more to work with.

Other Exercises for Clairaudience

- Guess what song is going to come on the radio next.
- Meditate on a question. Ask it while in a meditative state and see what answer pops up in your clairaudient hearing.
- With a friend, choose ten keywords. While in different locations (where you can't hear each other), take turns saying one of the words out loud. See if you can "hear" which word your friend said.

TRY IT OUT

Follow the steps described to enhance your clairaudient abilities. Record your answers to these questions to reflect on your experience:

+ How can I discern between psychic hearing and my own hearing?
+ Has there been a time when I "heard" a message in my head?
+ How else have I been practicing clairaudience without realizing it?
+ When in my life has guidance come to me in the form of clairaudient messages? Were they difficult to isolate?
+ How do I want to practice this gift?

13 Develop Your Clear Smelling

Have you ever gotten a strong scent of your late grandmother's perfume coming from seemingly out of nowhere? Do you ever smell flowers in spaces that have none? As you learned in Part 1, psychic smelling, or "clairalience," is a gift that you can expand in order to receive messages from loved ones on the other side and from celestial beings such as angels. Because it feels like actual smelling, it's easy to brush off these intense psychic signals as coincidence or a fond memory. In actuality, these are calling cards from the other side to get your attention!

If you have always had a sensitive nose, you may already be using this ability without realizing it. Clairalience can manifest in many forms. Some psychics who specialize in this skill can even "smell" death before it happens. They tend to associate an impending passing with a smell they cannot quite describe; it is unlike anything familiar. You may also be able to smell the energies of events, emotions, thoughts, and more (e.g., smelling lavender when someone near you is going to find love soon).

A more common way you'll be able to experience psychic smelling is through messages from angels and loved ones on the other side. Angels often have a floral, pleasant scent they send for support and awareness. Loved ones on the other side who are trying to make a connection with you, or want you to give a message to someone else, will deliver a smell of their signature cigar or the morning cup of steaming black coffee they faithfully enjoyed in life.

GETTING READY

To prepare to stretch your clairalience muscles, choose an essential oil you are familiar with that calms you. Lavender or rose are wonderful beginner scents. Find a quiet place without other strong smells that can distract you. Use the script provided in Part 1 or your preferred method to get into a meditative state, paying particular attention to your throat chakra.

How to Practice Clear Smelling

1. Once in a meditative state, smell your chosen essential oil for a moment. Breathe it in through your nose and hold the oil by your nose for a few seconds. As you breathe out through your mouth, imagine the scent is staying with you, imprinting its energies into your soul. Your third eye may awaken here, especially if you are closing your eyes. Take note of what you see, if anything.

2. Think of the scent and how it smelled. Without holding it by your nose, focus on your throat chakra and re-create the smell.

3. When you can no longer hold this focus, smell the oil again.

4. Again, without holding the oil by your nose, focus on your throat chakra and re-create the smell.

5. Repeat steps three and four for about ten minutes, until you really feel comfortable with the exercise.

6. After the initial introduction to the exercise, take a moment to informally re-create the smell as you find yourself feeling relaxed throughout various moments of your day. In a meditative state, you can even re-create it without the oil in front of you, using your throat chakra to assist you.

In time, you will find that not only can you very strongly and convincingly re-create the scent for yourself whenever you want; you can also now differentiate between an actual smell and one that you are "remembering."

Further Practice

Now that you are understanding your psychic smell, start noticing all the smells around you. Talk about them with others. See if they can smell the same things you can. You may not have realized that a lot of what you have been smelling, and will smell, is not a shared experience. You have most likely been noticing scents your entire life that are indications of psychic messages! For more practice, you can also:

- Meditate using other oils. Every time you try a new oil, you are expanding your gift, growing it, and making it stronger.
- Start to notice certain scents surrounding events and emotions. Funerals, weddings, birthdays, and conflicts can all be accompanied by distinct smells that are emitted from the energy produced by those situations. Having increased attention and self-awareness during these times will kick-start your ability to associate scents with events and emotions.

TRY IT OUT

Follow the steps described to explore and enhance your clairalient abilities. Record your answers to these questions to reflect on your experience:

✦ What did I see in my third eye, if anything, when I meditated with the oil?
✦ What smells have seemingly come from nowhere in my life? What might they have meant?
✦ Am I particularly sensitive to smells?
✦ Do I feel I can taste certain things when I smell them? What are they, and how do they taste?
✦ What am I going to do moving forward to increase my clear smelling self-awareness?

14 Send a Telepathic Text

Have you ever thought of someone, then they suddenly called you? After feeling like you had seen someone, did you run into them later that day? Telepathic communication is a skill we all have, and when it's strengthened, it can be used to communicate effectively with people who aren't physically near you.

Telepathy is the ability to transmit information from one person to another without using any means of "normal" human interaction. Everyone can do this; in fact, you engage telepathically via the subconscious all the time. There are different forms of telepathy, but it all boils down to the act of communicating with someone else's Higher Self via your own Higher Self.

Every time you have a psychic bond with someone, telepathic communication is possible. Psychic bonds occur in pre-existing mutual relationships. These are your connections with friends, family members, and anyone you have a relationship with. Some psychic bonds are stronger than others. You and your best friend will have a stronger psychic bond than you and someone you casually met at a party. People you don't always speak to day-to-day can also have a psychic bond with you, like an extended family member or an ex–significant other you didn't find closure with.

Telepathic communication at first can feel like thinking about someone. They enter into your mind seemingly at random, or you feel compelled to reach out with a misplaced urgency. This can be a strong indication that they are pulling on the psychic bond you share. Likewise, you can learn to send telepathic messages to others you share a bond with, giving them information, comfort, and love by controlling the energy you send.

Telepathy can also occur via dreams. You may have a dream about someone and the next day you hear they had some sort of conflict or major situation occur. You may notice when on the phone with one family member, other family members start to call in and make contact at the same time. You may have a conversation telepathically with a friend about a television show you are both watching, or you may simply know what they are going through and thinking without ever making physical contact.

GETTING READY

Choosing a person who is ready to practice telepathy with you is essential for this activity. You want to have an established psychic bond with a person who feels open to the experience. This is the "key" to their energy space. Between the two of you, decide on a day that you will both send a message to one another. You won't know the exact moment the other person will be sending out their telepathic "text," but you will know it's going to be sometime within that twenty-four-hour time slot.

How to Telepathically Text

1. When you are ready, choose a time and really record that moment in your mind's eye. Use your mind's imagination, picturing the time in an over-the-top way—perhaps on a huge scoreboard or in some sort of glitter lights!

2. Sit in a quiet space and picture the other person sitting in front of you. Try to really visualize not just their physical appearance but also how they make you feel when you are with them. Picture yourself typing out a text to them, envisioning the message letter by letter. Keep it short, and make sure you assign a feeling to the text you are sending. If they don't receive the

actual message at first, they still may be able to pick up on the overall intention. If you are a more visual person, picture sending an emoji to go along with your text.

3. Now, picture yourself hitting the send button, and envision them picking up their phone and looking down to see it. See them reading it.

4. As you end the exercise, feel gratitude and love for this person in your life. Don't forget to follow up at the end of the twenty-four hours to see if they got the message, and whether you received theirs!

The more you practice this with a friend, the more you will be able to really hone your telepathic giving and receiving skills.

TRY IT OUT

Follow the steps described to send a telepathic text. Record your answers to these questions to reflect on your experience:

+ What are some ways I feel telepathy during my day?
+ How would I describe the telepathic texting experience with my friend?
+ What did I see that surprised me during the psychic texting session?
+ What feelings were correct that I received? What feelings were incorrect?
+ What feelings surrounded each correct and incorrect feeling?

ACTIVITY

15 Channel Spirit in Your Art

Have you ever found yourself mindlessly drawing, only to look down and be surprised by what you see? Do you enjoy doodling in order to pay attention in meetings, classes, or long lectures? These are all forms of automatic drawing! When you allow your subconscious to take over in a mindful way, you can use this natural ability to channel important messages from Spirit to yourself and others.

Mediums and psychics can use automatic drawing to receive overall spirit guidance that can be missed with the spoken or written word. As you continue to practice your own psychic skills, you may find yourself wanting to draw or doodle as you meditate or ask for guidance. Sometimes psychics draw while giving readings and, as they do so, find answers hidden in the scribbles they have created. You do not need to have an advanced artistic ability to do this; however, those who are used to drawing, sketching, or painting may have an easier time putting aside their hesitations to jump into this practice.

GETTING READY

For this activity, you're going to need a quiet space, plenty of art supplies, and a subject to focus on. Maybe you are doing this automatic drawing practice in order to receive messages for yourself or for a friend. It's important to choose a general topic you are looking to understand, but keep the range wide open for whatever Spirit wants to say (at least when starting out). Topics can include messages your spirit guides would like you to know or what your Higher Self has to say. The key is letting go of control and drawing or painting from a power greater than your own. The medium you feel comfortable using may change. This, as in all psychic exercises, will take some trial and error. You can always switch up your sketching pad and charcoal pencil for a watercolor palette and canvas if it feels best for your practice. Follow your inner wisdom on this one! In fact, different subjects you choose to focus on during channeling sessions may inspire you to use different artistic mediums.

How to Perform Automatic Drawing/Painting

1. Begin in your meditative state, using the script in Part 1 or your preferred method.
2. Mindfully pick up the paintbrush, charcoal pencil, or whatever artistic tool you will be using to do the exercise. Begin to intently focus on it and, as you do, see your hand become part of it. Visualize your arm and your whole body becoming one with the tool you are holding.
3. Ask Spirit to use you the way you would use that art tool. You are now the paintbrush, charcoal pencil, etc. Your entire being is now being utilized to give this message.
4. You may want to enter a state of mind that is hypnotic and less open to outside influences. Repeat a mantra such as "I am message," or listen to meditative music that carries you away.
5. Let Spirit create its message through you. As you are making the art, it's okay to be curious about what you are drawing or painting, but practice not paying attention to it. You may want to close your eyes or stare with a soft gaze instead. There is no wrong way to do this, only the way you feel most comfortable and receptive.
6. When you feel the image is done, take a step back and release yourself from the visualization of being the artist's tool. You are

now you, and you can shake off any residual feelings of connection you may have by taking large, clearing breaths.

7. Look carefully at what you have created. What doesn't make sense to you now can make sense later. If the subject of the message is someone other than you, they may need to look at it and offer their own interpretations.

Check Your Ego
Over time, this practice will become more routine, and it will be easier to disengage your ego from your channeling. You should feel light, calm, and peaceful. If you feel anxious or stressed, simply take a step back from it. There is no need to "try" to do this; just flow with it. What you create may look like absolutely nothing at first, but over time, your adeptness to make shapes, color schemes, and hidden gems of messages will improve. Remember, you are the art medium and there is a larger force guiding you!

TRY IT OUT

Follow the steps described to perform an automatic art session. Record your answers to these questions to reflect on your experience:

+ What did I ask Spirit to focus on at the beginning of the session?
+ What did I notice about my body when I was painting/drawing?
+ Where did my mind wander when I was feeling connected to the process?
+ What prompted my mind to wander to distracting thoughts during the activity?
+ What shapes do I tend to draw during this practice?
+ What style does this art piece remind me of?

16 Channel Spirit in Writing

Have you ever zoned out and written at the same time? Automatic writing is a great way to tap into your Higher Self to receive helpful messages by creating a flow of information between your highest good and your physical self. There is a deep pool of limitless knowledge ready for you to draw from—and it's inside you. Your Higher Self has awareness of what you have come to this world for, where the lessons you are learning will take you, and how to move forward in the best way to fulfill your soul contract.

Tapping into a stream of consciousness and seeing what shows up on paper can be quite surprising and powerful. The writings that can come to you during these sessions can be helpful to your overall growth, give you insight into a challenge you are currently undergoing, or just give you support and suggestions for your future endeavors. You can use these messages generated through automatic writing as part of your daily meditation practice or in sessions where you connect with Spirit.

GETTING READY

Find a comfortable place to write and a pen/pencil and journal. A large journal with ample space is preferable, as you may be closing your eyes during this exercise. Be sure your chosen space has few distractions.

In this space, focus on a specific question and direct it toward your Higher Self and spirit guides. You may have a bigger life question, like "What is my purpose here?" Or, if you want to seek guidance on a certain situation, you may ask something like "What choice do I need to make?" Write this question at the top of the page in your journal for focus and later reference.

The real trick of automatic writing is the ability to clear the mind. With devoted practice, you can learn to separate your conscious thought from your connection to Spirit and self. Think of yourself as the observer of what is happening around you. You are part of it but watching as if you are sitting far from what is happening. You will find this exercise easier to engage in if you approach it with curiosity and quiet observation.

Check Your Senses

Focus on your physical feelings throughout this activity. You should be feeling light and perhaps even a little "floaty." You may feel tired or even distracted by other thoughts. As your hand moves, you may feel detached from it, but in a peaceful and calm way. Deep breathing and repeating a mantra such as "I am message" can help you stay focused. Also, listening to meditative music during this practice can help.

How to Perform Automatic Writing

1. Enter a quiet and meditative state in your chosen space, using the script in Part 1 or your preferred method.
2. Close your eyes (if they aren't already closed) or look with a soft gaze and allow your pen/pencil to touch the paper and begin to move. Loosen up your hand a bit and simply allow it to feel moved by another force.
3. Try not to lift your pen/pencil from the paper during this activity. Allow for a continuous stream of writing to emerge from your hand without ever looking directly at what you are producing or breaking contact from the energy between pen/pencil

and paper. (You may choose to type on a computer instead of writing. The setup is the same: Simply allow your fingers to move continuously on the keyboard.)

4. As soon as you feel disconnected, allow your pen/pencil to fall from the paper, or move your hands away from the keyboard, and know you are done.

More Practice
Immediately before entering your meditative state, write a name of someone you would like to focus on during the writing session. As you intentionally form each letter of their name, feel yourself connecting to their energy. You can also do this with names of places, events, or even questions. As you write your chosen words, ask Spirit to give you messages about them.

5. Use the meditation script in Part 1 to enter a meditative state.

6. Begin to put your pen to paper. If you find yourself feeling too involved in the writing process, rather than being guided to write, or guessing ahead at what you are writing, it's time to take a moment and recenter yourself. Remember to observe, not interact!

7. When you find it increasingly difficult to hold focus, you will know it's time to end the session. With time and practice, your endurance will improve.

You'll find that you will eventually be able to spend longer sessions in the right meditative mindset to do automatic writing, but practice is necessary! Try to be patient with yourself.

TRY IT OUT

Follow the steps described to perform automatic writing. Record your answers to these questions to reflect on your experience:

+ What distracted me when writing?
+ What engaged me when writing?
+ When my hand was moving effortlessly, what did I feel?
+ At what times did I feel a natural flow to my guided writing?
+ What did I see or think of during inspired moments?

17 Manifest an Intention

Everything is energy. All your thoughts, intentions, and feelings give off vibrations. These vibrations attract the opportunities, events, and people into your life that create your reality. By understanding how these energies work, and working with them instead of against them, you can make the most out of this abundant source of power. In this way, nothing that is intended for you in this lifetime is out of reach.

GETTING READY

Manifesting your desires requires an understanding of what it is you want, shaped into an "intention." An intention is the clear statement of what you want. When creating an intention, make it about an overall goal or feeling. It's important to be specific but not so specific that you limit the way it will be sent to you.

Tips for Creating an Intention

✦ Focus on what you want, not what you do not want; e.g., "I am financially abundant."

✦ Form your statement as if it has already happened; e.g., "My life is filled with love."

✦ Utilize the phrases "I am" or "I am able to"; e.g., "I am fulfilled and successful in my job."

✦ Do not use the phrase "I try"; e.g., "I try to be open and positive" becomes "I am open and positive."

+ Use gratitude in your statement; e.g., "I am grateful for friendship in my life/I am surrounded by people who care for me."
+ Make it believable to you; e.g., "I am open to love/I am willing to receive abundance."
+ Use this intention in your daily life! Watch your words in all conversations and self-talk; e.g., "I don't know how to do this" becomes "I am able to learn new things!"

After you've decided on your intention, write it down on sticky notes and place the notes where you will see them daily: your car, bathroom mirror, office computer, phone wallpaper, etc.

You will also need a plant, seed or seedling, a pot, and some soil for this activity.

How to Grow Your Intention

1. Write your intention on a small piece of paper.
2. Place it with the plant, seed, or seedling in the pot with the soil, lovingly stating your intention as you plant it.
3. Place this pot where you will see it daily and care for it as you would any plant you have in your home.

Every time you water the plant, gaze upon it, or check that it's doing well, you are giving beautiful energy to your intention. You are nurturing your intention, giving it to the universe to watch it grow, and carrying faith that it will in fact grow. Every time you plant a seed, you know you have to let nature take its course for it to grow. And when you plant an intention, you, too, have to allow the universe to take it and allow it to grow with faith and love.

As the plant grows, state your intention often and with gratitude that it has become your reality. The most precious thing about this activity is that when it does come to fruition, you'll find that you have already aligned yourself to it. When it enters your life, you will have already felt its presence long before its confirmation.

Check Your Ego

This is an intention you most likely are very connected to—one that you feel you need very much in order to live a happier and more fulfilled life. But you must let it go. Detachment is the hardest thing for our human egos to endure and practice. But just as when you plant a seed in the ground, you know there are some things you cannot do yourself. Things that you allow the force of something bigger than you to take care of. If you uncovered your seed every day to look at it, it would disrupt the process. It's the same with your intention. Repeating a mantra such as "I embrace peace" can be helpful in your detachment.

Of course, in addition to this practice, there will be times when you'll have to challenge yourself to manifest this desire. For example, when wanting a new job, you'll also have to get your resume ready and practice for interviews. When wanting a new romance, you'll also have to set out on some blind dates and embrace awkward first encounters. Sometimes you may find yourself at an impasse and have to switch up your game plan. The point is, expect some work.

TRY IT OUT

Follow the steps described to grow an intention and enhance your psychic powers of manifestation. Record your answers to these questions to reflect on your experience:

+ **What is my intention?**
+ **How does this express what I want in a positive and open-ended way?**

+ How did I feel as I planted this intention?
+ As I take care of my plant, how do I feel connected to my intention?
+ What are the feelings and emotions I am surrounding myself with as I grow my intention?
+ What are some ways I need to detach from the outcome?

18 Choose a Crystal for Psychic Work

Crystals have been highly regarded throughout time for their beauty and symbolism. The stones themselves are thought to be infused with specialized properties in which vibrations can flow and become aligned in various ways. Different crystals have various innate abilities to help you achieve the goals you set for yourself in your life and psychic practices. They can serve as holders of your intentions, reminders of your lessons learned, representations of the boundaries you have placed around yourself for support and protection, and more.

When choosing a crystal for a psychic practice, you will find that you inexplicably become pulled to a certain crystal for more reasons than just how it looks. You may find yourself drawn to certain crystals with an intuitive knowing. Letting a crystal choose you is a fun and introspective way to understand more about what you may need to be working on. Allowing your intuitive self to choose a crystal can help you look inward and deepen the psychic journey within.

GETTING READY

Now that you are well on your way in your psychic practice, you may already be aware of a local crystal shop in your area that provides a wide selection of raw and polished crystals. You will want to ensure that the stones you use are ethically sourced and produced; this makes a huge difference in how well they will function for you. You will also want to have an open mind and be ready to allow your intuitive self to do the shopping.

If you do not have a local store you can physically go to, you can do this practice online. There are many reputable retailers of crystals available.

How to Choose a Crystal

1. **When shopping in person:** Begin in an open and calm state, breathing steadily and feeling present in this moment.

2. If you are shopping in a store, simply walk around the crystals and take in what you see. Observe the crystals in a subjective manner. Try not to look at appearance; rather, see how each crystal makes you feel. As you do this, you may find that a certain crystal pulls your attention toward it.

3. Without second-guessing this natural curiosity, go toward it and see how you want to interact with it. You should feel inspired, interested, and almost as if you "know" this crystal already. It can feel as if, in a room of strangers, you found someone who is noticing you. Finding the crystal that chooses you is a lot like making a new friend.

4. If you feel it's right, pick up the stone. Pay attention to how you feel holding it. You may feel a charge or a recognition. Note what the stone is typically used for and what its properties are said to assist with. This will have something to do with a need in your life right now. By letting the crystal choose you, you can see what it has to say about the intentions you perhaps should be focusing on.

5. **When shopping online:** Center on one crystal shop or seller that feels right to you.

6. As you scan the online pages of available crystals, take note of which crystals draw you in. They may not be the most beautiful crystals; rather, they may just spark a question within you.

7. Stop on a crystal's image that captures you and picture yourself picking it up off the screen in front of you. Does it feel

"correct" in some way? Feel its texture in your hands and visualize it in your third eye (see the "Open Your Third Eye" activity), turning it over and looking at it up close.

8. When you purchase this crystal and take it home, you may wish to wait a few days before deciding what you want to do with it. You may want to program it as detailed in the "Program a Crystal" activity to understand more about what it's meant for in your life and journey. Crystals usually enter with a purpose that is needed in the present moment. Processing what that purpose is will be part of your personal reflection in the days ahead.

9. Get close to your crystal by having another person hide it in a room and finding it using the tips detailed in the "Practice Remote Viewing" activity. Your crystal has a special bond with you, which makes it easier to do this activity.

TRY IT OUT

Follow the steps described to choose a crystal for psychic work. Record your answers to these questions to reflect on your experience:

+ What did you feel entering the space or website with the crystals?
+ In what ways did this stone draw you in?
+ What is the meaning associated with the stone you chose?
+ How does this meaning apply to your life as of today?
+ When you hold the stone, how does it feel energetically within your body?

19 Read a Picture's Energy

Why did you swipe right or left on that online dating profile you just saw? Why did looking at the photos of local dentists make it easier to choose one? We are always energetically scanning photos—we just aren't told it's a psychic skill!

Photos capture the essence of a person, their overall personality, and sometimes even the motives and intentions they have. You can feel so many things when you take a moment to energetically read a photo, things that are, in turn, useful in guiding your choices moving forward. Reading a picture's energy can help you determine the role this person plays or can play in your life. It can assist you with aligning your energy to theirs and determining your energetic compatibility.

GETTING READY

This exercise works best with a friend who is open minded and supportive of your psychic journey. To prepare, have this person show you a picture of someone they know. It's best to use a photo with good lighting, no filters, and one where you can clearly see eyes. Headshots, professional photo shoots, or "occasion" pictures such as portraits from weddings or graduations aren't the best choices for picture reading, as they can give off inauthentic energies because of the stress the person was under that day.

How to Energetically Read a Picture

1. Looking carefully at the photo, begin to scan your own emotions for keys to who this person is. Ask yourself these questions as you scan: Would you go to this person if you were hurt? Would this person be a good leader? Do they like to be in charge? Can they take a joke? Would they like to hear about your day?

2. Putting yourself in a vulnerable position as to how this person would interact with you and make you feel will result in their energetic reading. You can find out so much information just from answering these questions as you carefully scan your feelings while looking at this picture.

Other Things to Consider As You Are Reading the Photo

+ **Do they remind you of someone in your life?** If someone reminds you randomly of someone else you know, it's not just a coincidence or your mind running away with thoughts. Spirit will superimpose images over another image in an attempt to get you to see the parallels. If the picture you are looking at reminds you of your best friend's eccentric mom from middle school, chances are they have a lot in common.

Check Your Emotions
Feeling heavy or nauseous can indicate a toxic person. Feeling light and happy can indicate the opposite qualities. Physical feelings can arise looking at a person's photo as well. Notice parts of your body calling your attention; you could be picking up on their health issues. If you start to feel anxious or nervous, you could be experiencing the stress they currently have in their life.

✦ **Do they look like a pop culture/historical figure or literary character?** Does this person look exactly like Harry Potter? They may have family issues and significant trauma related to familial relationships, like the fictional character. Do you think of a famous pop singer or a past president when you look at this person? Your spirit guides will use references such as these to get you to see parallels and symbolism. The cues aren't just random; they are specific pings from Spirit that carry important information.

✦ **Do you sense a relationship vibration?** Do you look at the picture and feel like they have a motherly energy? If it's a family picture, can you tell who the oldest sibling is? Spirit will often show family dynamics. Feeling like a sibling is the oldest or that a sibling is motherly is actually a way Spirit can tell you what's going on behind the scenes in the photo.

Check Your Ego

"Cold reading" is when a person takes logical cues and creates mystical meaning out of them. As a psychic, you want to avoid this tactic, as it's not true to what you are doing in a psychic practice. It's normal to pay attention to age, race, clothing, and overall physical appearance, but make sure you go beneath the cover of someone's image into their actual energetic self. You aren't reading their obvious cues: You are picking up their emotions, their vibrational waves, and their essence as a person. This takes practice, but you will find that not many people are how they appear.

TRY IT OUT

Follow the steps described to energetically read a picture.
Check in with the source who can confirm what insights you've
gathered. Record your answers to these questions to reflect on
your experience:

+ What emotions did I feel while looking at the picture?
+ Where could I feel a distinction between my own feelings and
  another energy?
+ Which questions did I ask that helped me the most in reading
  the picture?
+ How do I feel about this person having read their picture?
+ What surprised me about this exercise?

20 Receive Messages from Objects

When holding an old piece of jewelry, have you ever felt more than just the item in your hand? Objects carry energy; the more emotional (meaning the more personal) an object is, the more powerful the vibrations emitted. We can interpret these frequencies when we attune ourselves to them. Psychometry is the psychic ability to read an object and "see" the history it has within. Psychics can do this when holding the object in their hands or touching it to their third eye. You can immediately sense certain tastes, smells, visions, and emotions that come with the object. Holding the wallet of a deceased relative may give you impressions of their daily life. Handling a wedding dress can give you imprinted images of the day it was worn and thoughts or emotions of the person who wore it.

With time and practice, you can hear the unique tales that different objects tell. Metal is an especially good conduit for spirit messages and impressed energies from long ago. For this reason, jewelry that was worn often by someone can be a wonderful object to interpret during this activity. Many psychics use psychometry to connect loved ones to those who have crossed over or bring closure to a question that has remained unanswered.

GETTING READY

For this exercise, you will want a piece of jewelry you know nothing about, but one that has been very near and dear to someone's heart. This works best with a friend or relative, someone you have a strong bond with and who is open to assisting you with your psychic development. This person should know about the item they are lending to you to interpret and be able to confirm the energies you receive. They will need to take notes on what you say as you interpret the object so you can look back and reflect on them later.

How to Perform an Object Interpretation

1. Begin in a meditative state, using the script in Part 1 or your preferred method.
2. Close your eyes if you haven't already. Without physically seeing the object, allow the person with you to hand it to you. It's very important you don't look at it, especially when starting to perform this activity. Your physical eyes can take away from your ability to really see the object in its energetic light.
3. Introduce yourself to this object and its energies by putting your hand on it softly and greeting it (either in your head or out loud), just as you would greet a person. You are about to have a conversation with it, and being polite opens up the portals to do so more easily. The vulnerable connection you create will facilitate stronger messages.
4. Have a friend ready to take notes or a recording device ready to go.
5. In your third eye vision (refer to the "Open Your Third Eye" and "Balance Your Chakras" activities for more information), see what appears to you. Without censoring yourself, simply begin speaking what you see. Even if it's nothing, start by saying that you are not seeing anything yet. Spirit will lead your voice as you open up your throat chakra in this way.
6. As you freely speak, you will "see" visions. It is okay if they are blurry and fleeting at first. Just describe them. It is important to note that you may not initially understand what you pick up

from the object. Your task is simply to report everything you can, regardless of whether it makes sense or not.

7. Complete a scan of your senses to gather more about what you are picking up. Do you smell, taste, or feel anything? You may start to get shadow pains in parts of your body or a feeling of fabric draping over you. Scan your emotions as well, stating how you feel while holding this object. Do you have a longing for someone you don't quite know? Or perhaps you feel joyful or in love.

End this activity by thanking the energy surrounding the object. Allow the visions to leave your mind, and your energy to come back into you.

You will want to follow up by immediately listening to, reflecting upon, and (if you find it helpful) transcribing the notes or audio recordings that were taken during the interpretation.

TRY IT OUT

Follow the steps described to perform an object interpretation. Record your answers to these questions to reflect on your experience:

+ What did I feel when I was handed the object?
+ How long did it take to "see" and "feel" sensations?
+ How did these visions and sensations emerge?
+ When did the flow of what I sensed become more rapid?
+ When did this flow slow down?

21 Do a Palm Reading

Do you believe that your personality, fate, and love are all pre-recorded on your palm? Palmistry is an ancient practice of looking at lines on the palm to enlighten others on their strengths, weaknesses, and the roads that lie ahead in their life. Think of palmistry as a map to a person's potential. Giving insight to someone through palmistry can be an amazing way to connect that person to their own self and uncover the roadblocks that may get in the way of what they want.

GETTING READY

You will want a journal at all times when doing a palm reading. As you go about your journey, your palmistry journal will allow you to write and draw what you see and what you need to further study. You aren't just learning the lines and what they mean: You are learning how to interpret them in a way that the person can actually use and be inspired by.

How to Read Palms

The best palm to begin with is your own. So take a look at your right palm and use the information provided here to start reading! Get out a journal and record what you see and what you need to learn more about. Afterward, you can continue this practice with friendly volunteers.

Main Lines

+ **Head line (center of the palm).** This line deals with your intelligence, mental health, and emotional well-being. A clear line that is flat and without breaks indicates a logical and direct thinker. Longer lines say you are able to retain information and have a natural inclination toward lifelong learning. A shorter line means you are quick to make choices and impulsive about decision-making. A deeper line suggests you have a good memory, while a lighter and fainter line says the opposite.

+ **Heart line (across the top of the palm).** The heart line deals with all matters of love in your life, including self-love, your style of love, and what types of relationships affect you. A curved line indicates a caring and empathetic approach toward relationships. If your heart line has little or no curve, it indicates a more passive approach to love. Longer lines indicate more exploration with love is in the future, and shorter ones suggest you are less likely to need variety in this area of life. If the line runs parallel to your head line, it means you have strong emotional control in all areas of love. You don't get carried away by your heart's desires.

+ **Life line (vertical beside the thumb).** The life line deals with your enthusiasm for life and the vitality you possess. The length of the line does not have anything to do with how long you will live! The depth, consistency, and marks on it are of importance. Beginning around the thumb, a chained or broken line means you had a rough start at life. How widely it rounds out into your palm is an indicator of how adventurous you are. A long life line signifies an ability to bounce back quickly from hardships.

+ **Fate line (vertical beside the life line, toward the pinkie finger side of the palm).** The fate line deals with how society, world events, and overall destiny have a hold on your life and its path. This line speaks to everything that happens to you that you have no control over. Where the line starts is significant. A line beginning at your wrist indicates many will know you, which can happen if you have a job that connects you to many people. If the line starts at your head line, it can indicate things will happen for you later in life.

Rare Lines

+ **Girdle of Venus (above the heart line, between the middle two fingers).** This line shows that you have an amazing ability to connect with people on a spiritual level. You are incredibly emotionally intelligent and able to put this to use for your highest advantage.
+ **Intuition line (vertical, below the pinkie finger).** The intuition line is an indicator of how connected you are to your intuition. Having this line means you are a natural medium and conduit of spirit voices and messages.
+ **Bracelet lines (the base of the wrist).** Also known as "rascette" lines, these lines are said to foretell health and wealth! Most people have three bracelet lines. More than three indicate a very fulfilling life. Fewer than three lines can indicate that happiness is something you have to really work on; finding contentment with what you have can be a challenge.

TRY IT OUT

Follow the steps described to perform palmistry. Record your answers to these questions to reflect on your experience:

+ Did you get any other energetic sensations while looking at someone's palm?
+ As you learn more about the lines, what connections do you feel exist between them?
+ Which lines do you need to explore more?

22 Program a Crystal

Everyone needs support in life. As you navigate life and your goals, you need little reminders of the energy you carry with you and the intentions in your heart. Programming a crystal to carry an intention is an easy way to provide scaffolding to your dreams and objectives when life makes things a bit unstable or shaky. When working in the psychic realms with different energies coming at you, crystals can be particularly great tools for stabilizing yourself, grounding your energy, and reconnecting with what this work is really all about.

When you use your programmed crystal, you will have a powerful tool for reminding yourself what your intentions are. When you feel like you have forgotten yourself or your purpose, it's a beautiful guiding light. You'll end up having quite a few of these kinds of tools around your sacred spaces, and it's normal to get a bit attached to them! These are your support systems, your powerful helpers as you move inward along your psychic journey.

Crystals want to be programmed; they are perfectly made for it. Every crystal has its own molecular makeup and vibrational frequency that allows it to hold and channel directed energy. Finding a crystal that complies with your intention is a great place to begin. Rose quartz, for example, is aligned to help with all things love and emotional healing, while amethyst has powerful mood-balancing properties.

GETTING READY

To begin, you may want to complete the "Choose a Crystal for Psychic Work" activity. Otherwise, some good stones for any intention are clear quartz, aura quartz, or rainbow moonstone. Once you have your perfect crystal, it will be time to create your intention. Back in the "Manifest an Intention" activity, you learned how to construct a strong and useful intention. Revisit that exercise for reference if need be. Write your intention on a piece of paper and sit in a cozy and relaxed space with your crystal. Under the moonlight or in natural sunlight can be very comfortable.

How to Program Your Crystal

1. In the space where you feel comfortable, with your intention ready, hold your crystal in your hands. Feel its edges and pay special attention to the details you can make out as you explore its surface with your fingertips.

2. Feel a natural curiosity about the crystal. As you hold it in the palm of your hand, feel any frequencies it radiates out to you. Does it make you feel calm or anxious? Does it feel healing or inquisitive? Is it a powerful stone that feels protective or a gentle stone that feels peaceful? The purpose of this is to get to know your crystal and feel it getting to know you as well.

3. When you feel ready, hold your crystal to your third eye chakra (the space between your eyebrows).

4. Start to repeat your intention out loud and, as you do so, feel the energy from your third eye imprinting this intention onto the crystal itself. You are programming the crystal with your intention, taking your pure desire and soul want and imprinting it on the crystal. It's as if you are handing off this desire and placing it in the crystal to be stored, kept safe, and honored. You may hold this crystal to your third eye chakra for as long

as you want. You will know when it has been programmed sufficiently.

5. When your crystal is programmed, you may feel lighter, calmer. You may even feel emotional because you have taken something so near and dear to you and transferred it to this crystal. You may feel unburdened. The crystal itself is now carrying your want for you.

6. When you are feeling lost, unbalanced, or distraught, holding this crystal will align you back to your original intention and the beautiful frequency and vibration your intention carries.

Keep your crystals away from too much sunlight and from other crystals. Depending on which crystal you have, there are different ways to cleanse it and keep it safe.

TRY IT OUT

Follow the steps described to program a crystal. Record your answers to these questions to reflect on your experience:

+ Why did I choose my crystal?
+ What did I feel holding the crystal before programming it?
+ What did I feel holding the crystal after programming it?
+ How did it feel during the programming?
+ What images did I see and emotions did I experience while programming my crystal?

23 Receive Messages from Ancestral Photos

The psychic bonds you have with your ancestors are very strong and invested. The sacrifices they made and the energy they put forth in their lifetimes so that you could benefit are things that surround you right now. Tapping into that bond is something you are able to do, and reading old family photos is a wonderful way to do so. Photos (and items) from those who have gone before you can connect you to their energy. Energy does not die; it simply changes form. The love that fueled your ancestors' ambitions is an energy that you can channel.

Mediumship is the ability to connect to those who have crossed over. It's always easier to channel the ones you have psychic bonds with already. Family members you have never met, the ones who are several generations back, can be communicated with in this way. You will get messages from their photos through emotions and your third eye visualization. You will be using all your psychic clairs to do this, starting with an intention of connection, love, and gratitude.

GETTING READY

It's time to gather some old family photos, artifacts, and histories. If you don't already have them, reach out to someone in your family who does, or turn to ancestral websites and archival resources. This part may require some digging and investigation. During this research and gathering phase, notice how you feel, what messages you get, and what inspires you. Take note of what songs come up on the radio, which periods of history you feel drawn to, and what names and dates stand out to you. The moment you begin this journey, your ancestors will be speaking with you, tugging at your attention, and getting you to hear them in various ways.

Once you get your timelines, photos, and artifacts, take your time choosing where you want to begin reading the photos. There may be a feeling of interest in one area of the family more than another at first. Follow your curiosity, as this is how Spirit directs you. If you are having fun and feeling inspired, that's Spirit! It's okay if you don't know anything about the photos you are going to be reading; part of this process will involve you putting together information as you go along. When you fact-check the messages you get in this activity, you can provide yourself validation. You will also want a journal devoted to your memory keeping for this activity, and you should review the "Read a Picture's Energy" activity.

Finally, get into a meditative state. Use the script in Part 1 or your preferred method.

How to Read Family Photos

1. Begin in your meditative state with your three-word journal.
2. In your third eye vision (refer to the "Open Your Third Eye" and "Balance Your Chakras" activities for more information) and your physical vision, see what appears to you as you look over the photo. Pay very close attention to your physical and emotional feelings and how they may change. Do you find yourself suddenly concerned with a certain family member? Is there a feeling of pride or loss?
3. Ask out loud for the name(s) of whoever is in the photo. Write down whatever comes to you in response, whether these answers come in a vision, sound, emotion, or physical sensation.

4. Ask them out loud what other names are important to them. Again, write the answers you get.

5. Now you can ask deeper questions, like "What was your motivation in life?" "What was your life's work?" "Did you have children?" "How did you pass away?" "What message(s) do you have for me?" "What is important for the family to know?" Because you are family, your ancestor(s) will have a solid investment in you understanding what they did in life and why they did it. Asking questions centering around this theme is helpful in strengthening the quality of the messages you receive. Write down anything you see, hear, or feel in response to your deeper questions.

6. Once you are done, you can use what you wrote to fact-check the messages you received from the photo. Be sure to include what you find out in your journal as well. Try not to read more than two of these photos at a time. The energy can be exhausting when you are channeling messages from the other side. You may feel your ancestor(s) sticking with you afterward. Therefore, do not be surprised if they show up in dreams, start giving you symbols during the day, or even come up in conversation with other family members who aren't involved in your work.

TRY IT OUT

Follow the steps described to read messages from ancestral photos. Record your answers to these questions to reflect on your experience:

+ Where has my energy been pulled since beginning of practice?
+ What did it feel like to connect with the energy in the picture?
+ What did I see immediately?
+ What do I feel my ancestors' overall message was?
+ What do I intuitively feel my next project will be within this psychic skill?

24   Use Your Psychic Calendar

Time is an illusion of our earthly lives. The concept that we have of it, as well as its linear structure, is representative of our physical bodies, not our eternal souls. Our energy is as limitless and abundant as the universe itself. When trying to psychically pin down when a specific moment, event, or situation will occur, it's helpful to think of time as a segment of space and energy, rather than a set place on a timeline. When wanting to know a specific date for the future, or investigating happenings in the past and present, you'll need to think of time as a suggestion.

However, when you do want to pin down a date, season, or other chunk of time in order to add detail to a precognitive psychic message, you can create a "psychic calendar." A psychic calendar is simply a visualization exercise that uses your third eye sight to give you dates and times to work with in your psychic practices. Just like flipping through your paper desk calendar or scrolling through your phone's calendar app, this calendar will assist you in answering questions as you look into the future.

As you grow your psychic abilities, you will begin to get premonitions and flashes of future events and people more easily. Remember: You do not control the things that you see. They are not yours to change or manipulate, and you being able to see them is not what causes them to occur. It's also important to note that timing is subjective and in total accordance with free will. Free will is the variable in all psychic predictions. People have the power to change the future by making different choices. Therefore, no prediction of future timing can ever be fully accurate, since one can make different choices to change the course of what will happen.

GETTING READY

This is a visualization exercise of the third eye. You will want to have fully practiced the "Open Your Third Eye" activity before moving forward. Additionally, really take a moment to decide what your psychic calendar will look like. This is going to be a tool you use throughout your psychic journey. It's like going to the office supply store and picking out the calendar of your choice to keep on your desk, except in your third eye vision! It needs to represent and reflect you, so think about what details this calendar includes that reflect your personal style and preference.

This exercise pairs well with performing any sort of psychic predictions (explained in more detail in the "Test Your Long-Term Psychic Predictions" activity). You can perform both exercises together, as you will need to focus on a particular person or past, present, or future event to complete this psychic calendar activity. Create a clear and well-defined question about when a certain event will happen.

Finally, get in a meditative state using the script in Part 1 or your preferred method.

How to Create a Psychic Calendar

1. In your meditative state, close your eyes and activate your third eye chakra using the steps in the "Open Your Third Eye" activity.
2. Picture your psychic calendar with your third eye. Feel yourself opening it and turning the pages. You may see the pages blur or even blend together at first, as if being flipped through rapidly.
3. Ask what year it is first (out loud), then look to the top of the calendar and take mental note of the first thing you see.
4. Ask the calendar to stop flipping and settle on when the event you are inquiring about will happen. Sometimes you may see a month with a date circled. You may see a few pages of the

calendar laid out, suggesting a period of time. Spirit also enjoys giving blocks of time in seasons, and if the answer you see in your third eye is not specific enough, you may ask for a chunk of time that is narrowed down. For example, you can ask, "Is this early, middle, or late fall?" and note what answer feels intuitively correct.

It's perfectly appropriate to ask a follow-up question with the calendar, especially if something isn't clear to you at first. You may ask for Spirit to repeat the timing answer or ask for a more specific date. You may ask if this will be surrounding a certain holiday or before or after another significant event. You may ask these follow-ups several times and flip back and forth between other questions you are asking Spirit to answer. Over time, the answers will become clearer, and flipping through your psychic calendar will be as natural to you as flipping through a physical calendar.

TRY IT OUT

Follow the steps described to create your psychic calendar. Record your answers to these questions to reflect on your experience:

+ What does my calendar look like?
+ How did my calendar move in my third eye visualization?
+ What question did I ask?
+ Did I ask a clarification question? What was it?
+ When my calendar stopped moving, what did I see?

25 Astral Project with Purpose

What would it feel like to free yourself from your physical form to explore the world around you? What if you were uninhibited by restrictions such as space and time? Astral traveling, or projection, is a way to step outside of these restrictions and travel whenever you want, to wherever you want!

This concept of being able to use your "astral body" to explore the "astral realm" is found in many cultures throughout history. The astral body is the conscious space you occupy between your physical body and soul body. The astral realm is a plane of existence that is not accessible by way of the physical body but can be visited by your astral body. It's how you are able to have out-of-body experiences and interact with realms of higher consciousness. The concept that we are more than the physical experience that ties us to our third-dimensional reality is one that fascinates and inspires us. The practice of astral projection is thought to give perspective and strengthen our connections with the universe. In the astral realm, you can connect with the Higher Selves of people in your life, have visitations with those who have crossed over, and interact with your spirit guides. You can visit the past, present, and future, and you can "see" events from a universal point of view.

If you've ever woken up with a start in a cold sweat needing a huge glass of water, you may have been astral traveling. People tend to write off unintentional astral projection as a wildly realistic dream. In this activity, you will intentionally travel through the astral realm.

GETTING READY

In order to astral project, you will have to hone a few other skills first. The ritual of meditating and aligning your consciousness to that of your Higher Self is one you should have down pat! Consistency and ease in these practices create the perfect space for astral projection.

Using crystals can also assist you with creating the alignment you need to begin the deep trance that is required for astral projection. Choose a crystal or two that creates comfort and peace within your being. Labradorite and citrine are excellent choices for astral travel. Labradorite promotes a sense of introspection and adventure, and citrine repels negative energy and fosters optimism. (See the "Choose a Crystal for Psychic Work" activity.)

Getting in the habit of recording your dreams in a dream journal is also necessary before practicing astral projection. The difference between typical dreams, lucid dreams (the state of being aware within a dream and being able to control what happens in that dream), and astral traveling will be more and more evident once you record and reflect on your dream experiences.

How to Astral Project

1. Get into a meditative state using the script in Part 1 or your preferred method.
2. In this state, picture yourself basking in a healing white light emanating from Source energy. You intuitively know it is the white protective light of the universe.
3. Within this white light, envision your astral body as a filmy essence that you are a part of. It is the "real" you beneath your physical features.

4. Picture the astral part of you rising up from your physical form, separating from your body. (This step may take some time to achieve.)
5. Once you are able to perform and maintain this visualization, practice turning your astral body to look at your physical body. Try to hold details of what you see for as long as you are able.
6. Once you can clearly see your physical body, you can use your astral body to explore rooms of your house and eventually other spaces entirely.

Tips for Astral Projection

+ **Try it while sleeping:** This is easier to do when you are sleeping; however, you have less control over where you go. Your subconscious will choose your direction!
+ **Don't judge your fear:** It's normal to feel panicked and fearful when astral traveling. You'll find that you are projecting, and then a realization rushes over you that you are separated from your body. You cannot "die" outside of your physical body; there is no danger to your physical body, and if you need to wake up at any point, it will happen immediately.
+ **Set your intention:** As you become better at your astral projection technique, state what your goals are for your astral projection. Perhaps they include a meeting with your spirit guides or a visit to the past, present, or future. Your intention could be to check on your relatives who live across the country or to receive a message from your Higher Self.

TRY IT OUT

Follow the steps described to astral project. Record your answers to these questions to reflect on your experience:

✦ How is astral projection different from meditation?
✦ How did I feel "leaving" my body?
✦ What made me break my concentration?
✦ What experiences did I have when astral projecting?
✦ How do I feel I can improve in this psychic skill?

26 Discover an Animal Messenger

Do you have a special affinity for a certain animal? Have you ever had a strange encounter with an animal that felt like more than just an experience with nature? Do you continuously see the same animal wherever you go, even in art? Cross culturally and throughout time, animals have held special symbolic meanings in spiritual practices. Spirit will use animals to deliver messages, give you a forewarning of what's to come, and as a reminder for what characteristics you need to honor and hold close to you as you grow. Sometimes animal messengers are sent for you to build awareness about your own strengths and weaknesses.

You may have an animal messenger that is consistent, and you also may see new ones periodically depending on what is going on in your life. Seeing an animal messenger will be accompanied by feelings of wonderment, joy, and connection. You can sense a deeper part of you awakening to what the appearance of this animal conveys.

Meetings with your animal messenger aren't just limited to literal in-the-flesh experiences. You may see this animal pop up in cards others give you, art you find yourself attracted to, and in other forms of media as well. Animal messengers tend to show up during times of transition and when you have questions that need answering. Becoming more aware of the symbolism of animals sent to you by Spirit will allow you to communicate more effectively with your guides and navigate your life's path.

GETTING READY

Thinking about what animals you tend to gravitate toward, reflect on what they mean to you. Your own symbolic interpretations are what your spirit guides will want you to focus on first when understanding what the messages mean. Animals are inherently inspiring to us for different reasons. Perhaps seeing a bear makes you feel comforted and creates an image of a cozy den or home. Or seeing a dolphin may make you feel free and full of joy. It may inspire you to remember that you are free to make the choices that serve you. You may wish to write about these animals in your spirit guide symbol book (see the "Create a Spirit Guide Symbol Book" activity), including the type of animal and the meaning it has for you. As you find new animals that you feel connected to, add them to your book.

Once you have explored your personal meanings, you can research different animals in more detail. Look to an animal's cultural significance in your ancestral lineage. You can also explore its literary significance and even astrological connections.

How to Discover Your Animal Messenger

1. Get into a meditative state using the script in Part 1 or your preferred method.
2. Focus on an animal that has special significance to you. Ask your spirit guides to give you the personal meaning it has for you. You will feel certain emotions and inspirations around this animal that are new and insightful.
3. Ask yourself what behaviors you find most inspiring, or most alarming, about this animal. What are the positive and negative connotations of this animal? Record all responses in your journal. You can also draw this animal if it comes naturally to you.

If this animal resonates with you and is particularly inspiring, take time to honor it. Come out of meditation and research its behaviors and environment. Consider bringing attention and awareness to any struggles it encounters in our world. If possible, donate time or money to helping this animal. This will further your connection with your guides and accelerate the symbolism this animal presents to you.

You may not always enjoy the feelings that come with an animal messenger. Perhaps it's an animal you associate with fear, distaste, or anxiety. Even if the animal isn't one you particularly enjoy, it doesn't make the message any less useful. Your animal messengers can help you explore your shadow side as well, or the wounded parts of you that tend to remain hidden from the conscious mind and are therefore more difficult to heal and mend.

TRY IT OUT

Follow the steps described to discover a personal animal messenger. Record your answers to these questions to reflect on your experience:

+ What does your animal messenger represent to you?
+ What negative or positive associations did you find in this animal?
+ What positive qualities of this animal messenger feel applicable in your life today?
+ What negative qualities of this animal messenger feel applicable in your life today?
+ What further activities can you do to connect with this symbolic energy?

ACTIVITY

27 Perform a House Cleansing and Blessing

Our space is important to us. And as we live in it, we fill it with not just knickknacks and furniture but also our energy and the energy of those who spend time with us. Because of this, periodically cleansing and blessing your space is important—especially as you are becoming more aware of your psychic sensitivities and abilities. The space you occupy needs to feel calm, neutral, and conducive to your psychic growth. The vibes that can pile up may causes blockages and heaviness that affect your skills.

There are different times when performing a cleansing and a blessing for either yourself or another person can be particularly beneficial. When you first move into a space, cleansing it of old energies that do not belong to you and performing a blessing will make you feel more at home. If you are feeling a heaviness after someone leaves your home, you may want to cleanse and bless the space so that any residue from their essence dissolves. When you are feeling anxious or stressed, cleansing and blessing your space can forge a clear path for accelerated healing, as new ideas, insight, and spiritual downloads arrive faster in a neutralized energetic atmosphere. Finally, just as you periodically clean your physical home, you'll find that energy, too, must be tidied up. The more you do it, the more you'll sense when it needs to be done.

GETTING READY

An intention must be in place before doing a cleansing and a blessing. The goal is to neutralize the energy. You will want to set an intention to cleanse any residue that no longer serves you and for the vibrations in the space to be clear, light, and neutral. Something like "This space is light and protected" works well as an intention, but you can use anything that resonates with you. Have your intention memorized and ready to repeat during the activity.

There are also a few tools you will need, and depending on how you develop your own style, you can add and rearrange whatever tools you'd like. Different religions and indigenous cultures have their own tools for cleansing and blessing a home; feel free to research your own culture and ancestral traditions. Asking for ancestral help is a lovely addition to a house cleansing and blessing. You may want to invest in a very high-quality herb spray for the practice as well. These are sold in reputable stores that specialize in cleansing and blessings materials. However, you can mix a spray yourself. For example, dissolving some essential oils such as lavender or lemon, or even a high-quality sea salt, in water works just as well. If there are certain scents that create tranquility within you, take that as a cue it's a helpful tool.

You'll also want a white candle for protection and some sort of instrument like a bell or singing bowl. If you don't have a bell or other instrument to use, clapping your hands works just as well. In addition, open a few doors and windows to let sunlight and fresh air in, and play music that calms and soothes you.

How to Perform a House Cleansing and Blessing

1. Light your candle while at the same time stating your intention out loud.

2. With your herb spray in hand, begin at the front of the house by your front door. Repeat your intention as you periodically spray your cleansing mist and make a sound with your chosen instrument or your hands.

3. Continue to walk through your home, stopping in front of every window and door and repeating step two. As you walk around, pay special attention to where the energy feels heavy or stuck. Spend a few moments anywhere else you intuitively feel the need to repeat step two. Don't forget corners and darker spaces. Spend time in space where you find yourself lost in thought or places that receive more negative energy than others. Places such as in front of the refrigerator, at the sink or stove, or at your desk need special attention.

When you feel the cleansing is complete, blow out the candle. As you do so, once again state your intention and intuitively ask for Spirit to bless this space with the white light of Source energy.

TRY IT OUT

Follow the steps described to cleanse and bless your home. Record your answers to these questions to reflect on your experience:

+ **What did your space feel like before the cleansing and blessing?**
+ **Where did you find yourself intuitively feeling the need to spend more time?**
+ **Which materials did you use that felt helpful? Why?**
+ **How does the space feel after the cleansing and blessing?**
+ **How can you sense the energy has shifted since the cleaning and blessing?**

28 Test Your Long-Term Psychic Predictions

The best way to grow your skill and confidence in your psychic abilities is to do a reading and test your long-term predictions! Before conducting a reading with another person, you will want to practice recording your psychic feelings, premonitions, and predictions in a journal. To begin, focus on a certain person, event, or world circumstance that has some time to play out. As you continue along your psychic journey, you'll notice that you have certain preferences and strengths. For example, some psychics are very gifted at predicting national or global news, while others concentrate on a particular individual's life. Being varied with your subjects and recording what messages you get in a journal will provide the framework and experience to reflect and figure out what areas of expertise are best suited for you. Having a journal of your long-term psychic predictions will help you keep track and gather insight as you test your abilities.

As you go along, keep in mind that as a psychic, you are not always supposed to understand what the messages you are receiving are about. Many times, you will receive symbols and messages that make no sense to you at first, but in time manifest as energetic forecasts that are highly accurate. Hindsight is actually the key to foresight! Understanding how it feels to receive a correct message, even when you don't know what it is about, creates your confidence in future readings.

GETTING READY

You will need a journal dedicated to your psychic predictions. This is also a great time to create a "reading space" for yourself. Visit the "Organize and Use Mystical Protection Tools" activity to learn how to create this space.

Before a psychic reading, clarify what it is you would like to focus on. Depending on how you personally connect to energy, you may need to use different tools as well. For example, if it is a person you are focusing on, having their name written out, a personal effect of theirs, or a picture of them may help. If you are focusing on an event, you may wish to be holding some sort of symbol attached to it, such as an invitation, graphic, or logo. If your reading is for a world circumstance, you may wish to have a map in front of you or pictures of flags or world leaders.

Write down several general questions ahead of time that you will ask Spirit about the person or situation, such as the outcome of an election years down the road, the trajectory of weather patterns across the globe, or perhaps the ten-year forecast for a person you are close to. Create these questions in an open-ended format to allow for a variety of answers.

How to Test Your Long-Term Psychic Predictions

1. Get in a meditative state using the script in Part 1 or your preferred method.
2. Say a prayer out loud that speaks to you. One that calls in white, protective light is a helpful start if you have not yet found your own prayer to use.
3. When you feel ready to ask for messages, open your journal to a blank page to prepare for what you receive.
4. Start asking your prepared list of questions out loud. Immediately write down whatever comes up in response without overthinking. You may also improvise and ask other questions as you

become more comfortable in the session. You may want to ask clarifying questions that help you understand a message you've received already. You could also ask for timelines by using your psychic calendar (see the "Use Your Psychic Calendar" activity).

Check Your Emotions
You may begin to feel sad, anxious, mad, or scared during the reading. These emotions are often answers and insight from Spirit. For example, asking about a global event and feeling frightened and upset can signify negative news. Whereas asking about a love connection and feeling joy can show that it is a good match!

5. When you intuitively feel the exercise has ended, breathe slowly and return to a present state of awareness. Date the entry.
6. Every few months, take time to reflect on earlier psychic predictions. This journal is meant to be used often but read less frequently. The longer time you give it between recording a reading and reviewing what messages you received, the better. Spirit can give messages that won't come to fruition for years. Review which messages feel correct and which ones are more fleeting.

TRY IT OUT

Follow the steps described to test your psychic predictions. Record your answers to these questions to reflect on your experience:

+ What words, phrases, feelings, or symbols came up?
+ What did you feel as you were connecting to your topic?
+ What was one prediction you felt particularly drawn to?
+ What did you receive that you did not understand?
+ Were there details that emerged that felt particularly strong? What were they?

29 Investigate Paranormal Activity

Have you ever been in a historic location and felt the vibrations of something...more? Something otherworldly? Do old houses feel different to you? When you open yourself up to the nuances of frequencies in your environment, energy from the past is hard to miss. Feeling suddenly at "home" in a place, or as if you are walking in someone else's personal space even if it's totally unoccupied, is not just your imagination. It's the vibrations of the past yearning to make contact with you.

The vibrations people can feel in their homes are like invisible roommates, rather than the powerful ghosts some envision when hearing the term "paranormal." These energies don't want to cause harm; they simply want to continue existing in the spaces that were significant to them during their lives. They are usually quiet and peaceful.

There are various reasons why the energy of those who have passed remains in the physical realm. Connecting with their energy is a way to find out why a particular energy is still here. In doing so, you can gather information about the history of the place you are studying, or you can provide an understanding so that you and the energy can coexist in peace.

In fact, there are benefits to having ghostly roommates! They are usually very protective of your house and can give off "vibes" to people you don't want in your space. They also can bring a sense of "home" to your environment so you feel very cozy and happy there, and everyone you invite can feel cozy and happy too. These energies add character and legacy to the place you call home.

GETTING READY

The intention when connecting with energies from the past is to understand what they want you to know and tell them what you can and cannot handle. If they have a message to give you, receiving it is the fastest way to calm them down. Take a look at the following tips to prepare for connecting with energy from the past:

✦ **Do your homework.** Research the space you feel is occupied by a ghost. Looking into the history of the home and the land around it can give you many cues as to who is with you and what their purpose is. Connecting with the energy will allow for better communication.

✦ **Be polite.** When you feel an energy around you that is foreign, it can feel as if you are being watched or walking into someone else's personal space. You may feel a rush of cold air or pick up a sudden scent in the air. In these cases, introduce yourself. Let the energy know who you are and state what your intentions are for entering the home. If you already live there, just say hello and let them know you acknowledge them but aren't in the mood for an interaction today! Say thank you and goodbye. Be firm. Remember, you are in control.

✦ **Watch the pets.** If you feel you're not alone, take a look at your pets. Is your cat on high alert too? Did your dog start staring at the wall and barking? Your animals sense otherworldly vibrations. Looking at the way your animals respond when you sense something otherworldly will confirm what you are picking up.

✦ **Record and listen.** There are a variety of paranormal devices you can use to communicate with ghosts. Some people use a tape recorder. Asking a question, letting the recorder run, and then playing it back to see what it picked up is one way to do this. What the human ear cannot hear, technology often can. Energy can use sound waves to create messages.

How to Investigate Paranormal Activity

1. Put yourself in a space that you feel is heavy with vibrations and get into a meditative state using the script in Part 1 or your preferred method.

2. Placing a mindful focus on your third eye chakra, ask any foreign vibrations to show themselves to you.

3. With all of your psychic senses in play, walk yourself around the room. Pay attention to how you feel, both emotionally and physically. Ask questions about who the vibration was in life and what this space meant to them. They may communicate through your emotions and sensations. Take careful note of what you see, hear, and feel.

Whenever you don't feel comfortable in your space, you can cleanse it. Refer back to the "Perform a House Cleansing and Blessing" activity for steps. Remember: This is your space and taking energetic ownership of it is completely okay.

TRY IT OUT

Follow the steps described to investigate paranormal activity. Record your answers to these questions to reflect on your experience:

+ What spaces in your life have you felt had a ghostly presence?
+ How was the energy different in these spaces?
+ How did you feel physically in these times?
+ What were some of the emotions that emerged while conducting the energetic interaction in this activity?
+ What do you intuitively feel the message of this energy to be?

30 Assign Colors to a Situation

Moments have moods. Moments have vibrations. The things that are not said are always lingering in the energy you pick up. Interpreting these moods can be done with your enhanced psychic intuition. One of the ways you can do this is by assigning colors to certain moods and vibrations you are experiencing.

Perhaps you are in the room during a tense conversation between coworkers and you sense the stress that exists. You can pick up on the chasm of energy colliding between these people. In this moment, assigning a color to the mood can help you better understand what the energy flow is. Perhaps you sense blue around the person who is feeling weaker, and red around the energy that is louder and more demanding. Over time, you will begin to develop a more automatic habit of assigning certain colors to certain moods and moments you observe. In this way, you can immediately see and understand what exactly is going on and, at times, what the result will be, simply by color coding the energy you feel.

Assigning colors can also help you label similar occurrences and patterns. You will be able to sense pink around true love, or purple around something that's fun for now but not long term. You will be able to associate blue with a compassionate endeavor and green at a time when what's going on is not personal to you at all.

GETTING READY

In the "Look for Auras" activity, you learned that every person has a unique energy signature around them. The colors listed there are similar to the colors you will want to assign to moments and experiences. The more familiar you become with associating colors with situations and people, the more you will be able to customize them to what makes the most sense to you. You will find that all colors come with connotations, negative and positive, depending on the context. For example, for a person on a power trip, yelling and showing disrespect to those they are supposed to lead, you may sense and assign red. But you may also find yourself assigning red to a moment of pure teamwork, with respected leadership that validates and assists those in the group. It's not about bad or good colors; it's about what they mean to you and how you apply and interpret them.

For the following exercise, you will want to place yourself in a spot where you can be a passive observer of people. You will want to be comfortable and calm in this space.

How to Assign Colors to Situations

1. Take three breaths in through your nose and out through your mouth.
2. Take a moment to calmly look at your surroundings. Envision yourself as the observer of them, rather than a direct participant, almost as if you are watching a movie in real time.
3. Now, look closer at what is happening around you and focus on a place you feel compelled to stay tuned in to.
4. Start to assign moods to the things you find yourself paying attention to. Does the conversation between the women feel intense? Does the hurried passerby feel anxious?
5. When you feel you have completed your observational writing and assigning of moods, start to think which colors come to

mind with each of the instances you took note of. Maybe the women's intense conversation feels red, and the hurried passerby feels yellow. Write down these colors beside the things you observed.

Doing this exercise several times a week for three to four weeks will give you enough instances to begin to see a pattern in the colors you assign to moods. They will start to have consistent significance.

Further Practice

At work, in family situations, and with friends, continue this practice. In time, this will become second nature to you. When something occurs, you'll automatically sense a color and realize what this energy is alluding to. You will be able to help those involved with a broadened perspective of what you feel is going on. In your psychic readings, hearing others' stories can also bring to mind colors. Eventually, this will be an effective way to confidently deliver messages to those who need them.

TRY IT OUT

Follow the steps described to assign colors to situations. Record your answers to these questions to reflect on your experience:

- ✦ What colors do I assign to different situations? Why?
- ✦ What color do I see most? What does it mean?
- ✦ Is there a color I associate with negative occurrences? Positive ones?
- ✦ What emotions and sensations come with assigning a color?
- ✦ Where and how can I use this ability moving forward?

31 Interpret Your Angel Numbers

As you move along your psychic journey, you will get many messages from your spirit guides. "Angel numbers" are a very popular kind of message from these high-vibrational beings. These are numeric codes designed to get your attention and either nudge you back to the places, mindsets, and choices that are in your best and highest interest or let you know that you are on the right track.

GETTING READY

The following are the meanings of the cardinal numbers used in angel numbers. Use these meanings to follow the steps for interpreting angel numbers.

✦ **0: Unconditional Love.** The force of love is around you all the time, taking the form of other people, opportunities, and even moments of clarity. This number enhances all attributes of the other numbers it appears with.

✦ **1: Architect.** Your world is shaped and altered by your thoughts and words. Right now, you are creating, and the powerful forces of the universe are working with you.

✦ **2: Trust.** It's not just the big things you can hope for; it's the little things that keep them all together. You are never alone, and your spirit guides are reminding you that so many small things together create a miraculous and cumulative outcome.

✦ **3: Harmony.** If something in your life is ignored or neglected, everything suffers. The health of the mind, body, and spirit connection is essential in living a fulfilled existence. Are you nurturing this connection?

✦ **4: Foundations.** There are things that, if left under nurtured, can fall to ruin. Seeing the number four reminds you to go to the foundations of self and take inventory of what is lacking. You can't build yourself up without maintaining all the good work you've already done.

✦ **5: Growth.** As you see the world around you shift and move, it's time to get flexible. Change is inevitable, and your peace comes not from the stability of things outside of you but from your foundation within.

✦ **6: Material World.** You are paying too much attention to the superficial. Oftentimes, you can forget the depth of what you are doing in life by focusing on the material world's distractions.

✦ **7: Fear Not.** Learning and growing come with new contexts and opportunities. You are feeling called to do new things without always knowing who or what to trust. This number reminds you to be spontaneous and courageous but also smart and cautious.

✦ **8: Abundance.** There are forces always flowing and moving through and around you. The ones you pay attention to and open up to will envelop you in their flow.

✦ **9: Endings.** In your life, something is coming to a completion. It can be sad, and it's okay to mourn what was, but it's also important to recognize the lesson in this ending as well.

How to Interpret Angel Numbers

1. **Break it down.** In a string of numbers, order is imperative! Cardinal numbers (single digits 0 to 9) are your keys to unlock the angelic message a number holds. The first digit in the sequence will point to the situation(s) that led you to this particular moment. The center digit gives you the core message of the entire sequence. The last digit will point to your likely future outcome. (If you are seeing just one or two digit numbers, the

meanings are more condensed to the present moment. If you are seeing four or five digits, think of it as your angels trying very hard to get your attention.)

2. **Check for master numbers.** There is an exception to the typical meaning of a number. Master numbers, or numbers that repeat, such as 11, 22, and so on, are not separated in the number's meaning. Rather, they are to be looked at as a whole number, with the meaning being an amplified version of the first digit.

3. **Use the number.** Once you have an idea of what an angel number presenting itself to you is about, start to communicate to your spirit guides with it. Take the number or numbers you repetitively see and draw them, use them in your screen names, or set a timer for that exact amount of time and meditate. You can donate money in the amount of your angel number and give denominations of this amount in tips or items. Using the number creatively in your daily life not only brings forth the energy the number represents, but also gets your angel guides' attention. When you start to communicate, they will get louder and stronger in their responses.

TRY IT OUT

Follow the steps described to look for and interpret angel numbers. Record your answers to these questions to reflect on your experience:

✦ What numbers do I consider my own, or "lucky"? Is it possible this has always been an angel number in disguise? Why or why not?

✦ What emotions do I get from my angel number?

✦ What does this number mean?

✦ How am I going to use my number to communicate with my spirit guides moving forward?

✦ How does this number relate in my life right now?

32 Send Someone Away Energetically

You have an innate ability to send your energy to someone as strongly as you are able to send your spoken words. After working with your natural telepathic abilities in the "Send a Telepathic Text" activity, you can start to use it in other ways as well.

Many times, as you become more sensitive to the energies around you, the energies can linger longer than you would like them to. You are already becoming more in tune to energy that is not yours yet makes itself known in and around you. Using telepathic energy to send others away energetically can assist you with feeling lighter and more yourself, vibrating with the authentic energy you need after tuning in to others' energies.

Owning your energy and creating boundaries around it is helpful not only for your psychic practice but also for your overall mood and health. In the past, you may have felt it rude to say goodbye to someone in a physical way and also subconsciously felt guilty about pushing their energy away. In actuality, just as it is healthy to move on from an interaction when it has reached a natural end or is becoming draining, letting someone's energy go when it no longer serves you is healthy for you—and that person. When you can no longer give your best version of yourself to another person, you owe it to them to say goodbye so that you can both move on in more beneficial relationships. You may feel you are thinking about this person too much, or their problems pop up a lot in your own interior dialogue. You may be having lamentations about the way things ended or be obsessing with what was left unsaid. You can also simply feel uncomfortable with their presence in your life and wish to distance yourself from it. Whatever your need to send away their energy, you can do so with grace and consideration for both of your needs.

GETTING READY

There are two ways you can approach the ability to send someone away energetically. You can do this in an actual physical experience or in a meditational one. When you are in conversations and interactions in person that are heavy, long lasting, or otherwise draining, sometimes the typical social cues to end it won't work. Telepathy can assist you with detaching from the energies of this situation.

Alternatively, there are times when you wish you could speak with someone again who you didn't have appropriate closure with. Perhaps it's a situation where you feel you can't reach out because it will not be handled well, or it's just not appropriate to do so anymore. The feelings and emotions can linger even though you know you cannot have the in-person conversation to amend it. Telepathy can help you speak to this person on a different plane, getting the closure needed to release that exhausting energy.

Pinpoint a time you can use this psychic activity and prepare yourself by utilizing the "Create a Protection Bubble" activity to get into a state of awareness of the energies you are impacted by. When you know you will be needing to send someone away energetically, you can quickly form this protective shield.

How to Send Someone Away Energetically

1. The next time you are in an inconvenient or uneasy conversation with someone that just won't end, send that person a

telepathic signal in your mind that they need to say goodbye *now*. You can smile and nod as they go on speaking, and as you do so, send the strong message: "Say goodbye; this conversation is over!" See how long it takes for them to wrap up and leave.

2. When a conversation cannot happen, but you wish to have closure with a person in your life who is impacting you energetically, telepathy can create healing communication. If you want to shut a door with someone, have a "goodbye" session with them in your head. You can say with love all the things you wish to say to them, and you can picture them also giving you their words and feelings back. Then send them on their way with love, compassionately telling their Higher Self it's time for this bond to be severed. In essence, you are having a conversation with their Higher Self. Having this conversation telepathically is going to help ease away their energy.

TRY IT OUT

Follow the steps described to send someone away energetically. Record your answers to these questions to reflect on your experience:

+ What person did I need closure with?
+ What did it feel like to connect telepathically with this person?
+ What emotions did I feel that I could sense were not my own?
+ How do I feel in the days after sending this energy away?
+ When do I feel stuck in situations where I could use telepathic energy moving forward?

33 Communicate with Pets

Energy is a universal language that people, animals, plants, and even objects can speak and understand. Using energy to communicate with animals is how you can perform a psychic pet reading! Animals are always picking up signals from you and the world around them. They don't question what they get; they simply trust. Their ability to sense impending events, threats, and even a trusting person who is offering help comes from their confidence in the energy that is all around them, energy that is full of information and messages. Animals are natural psychics! And they are ready and willing to connect with you.

Having a baseline understanding of how animals communicate is the first step in preparing to do a psychic pet reading. As humans, we tend to focus on the spoken word as our most fundamental and accurate communication tool. The word is where we get truth, what we are told to pay sole attention to, and where the foundation of our society sprouted. However, there is a world of meaning that lies in what is unsaid—a feeling, an intuitive connection, a vast knowing you cannot shake. Animals feel emotion and intention. They use it more than sound in order to understand the intention in an interaction. For example, you may say, "Sit!" to your dog, but when you speak it with insecurity because of a subconscious belief you will not be obeyed, the dog responds by jumping up instead. They hear your truth always, and this is what they will respond to. Similarly, two dogs may make growling noises when playing with each other but still understand the energy is friendly, unlike growls that mean "Back off!"

GETTING READY

Clearly stating your intentions and current emotional and physical state before sitting and spending time with an animal will help you understand what unintentional signals you are sending their way.

Animals will project images, physical feelings, and emotions to you during this practice. In your third eye vision, you may see something of importance to them. You will be using your sense of psychic smell, or "clairalience," to pick up important messages as well. Dogs especially communicate through smell, and sending you certain smell messages in this way is very common! You may also find yourself tasting certain things as you perform a reading. Psychic taste, or "clairgustance," is another unique yet normal way for animals to get their message across. Your "clairsentience," or clear feeling, will also be tapped into by animals. You may feel compelled to move a certain way, have a shadow pain in an area of your body, or even feel the urge to chew or bite something!

With an understanding of your intentions, energetic signature (the present emotional and physical state you are in), and how animals may be sending you signals, you are ready to begin your pet reading. For this exercise, pick an animal who is having some sort of behavioral issue. Perhaps it's a cat who isn't using their litter box or a dog who cannot stop barking when their owner leaves the house.

How to Perform a Pet Reading

1. Sit with the animal and enter a meditative state using the script in Part 1 or your preferred method. You may wish to close your eyes at times or simply have a soft stare in the animal's direction. Try not to force eye contact, as this can elicit anxiety.

2. Take time with this pet to feel its own vibration and attempt to match it. Breathe calmly, and simply enter the present moment of this animal's energy.

3. Ask a question directly to the animal, either out loud or in your head. Pay attention to your own body, mind, and emotions as you ask the question. Animals will often give you what they feel is important to know and not necessarily answer your questions.
4. Focus on what feelings you get in response. When you feel ideas entering your mind that are new, inspired, and clearly not yours, you will know you are picking up animal communication.

Check in once you have received feelings. If you felt a metallic taste in your mouth, for example, you will want to follow up on whether the pet is taking medication or what their water bowl is made of. You may feel a sense of insecurity from them, a feeling of not being useful. You may want to ask the owner if they seem bored or restless and what their daily activities are. The feelings and visuals you get are purely from the pet, but it will be up to you to put the pieces together for what the messages mean for the humans around them!

TRY IT OUT

Follow the steps described to perform a pet reading. Record your answers to these questions to reflect on your experience:

+ What did I feel emotionally from this animal?
+ Did I feel any physical feelings in my own body while doing the reading?
+ Did I receive any clairalience or clairgustance messages? What were they?
+ What do I think the pet was attempting to alert me to?
+ What surprised me the most about doing this reading?

34 Get In Touch with the Moon

There is a natural rhythm to this world—an ending and a beginning, a release and renewal. And this cyclical flow is shaped in part by the moon. The energy the moon releases controls tides, light, and more. Animals are influenced by it (for example, bird migrations are timed by it), and we, too, can feel the impact within us. The effects of the moon can be experienced in nuanced ways, and by paying attention to lunar cycles, you can harness that connection and feel the benefits of its power.

Moon cycles have long been part of human behavior, ceremony, and celebration. Each specific moon phase represents a counterpoint in our own being: a symbolic link that connects us to the natural flow of the lunar cycle. Linking your mood to the current moon phase can increase not only your self-awareness but also your spiritual responsibility; you release what is no longer needed and plant new intentions that honor your desired growth.

The moon is a tool you can use to become connected to self, Spirit, and this wondrous natural universe. And it begins with an understanding of each phase and its meaning.

Moon Phases and Meanings

+ **New Moon.** Explore your shadows in the darkness of the new moon. Taking time to journal, reflect, and figure out what it is you need to be focusing on is what the new moon empowers you to do. Write down your intentions for the upcoming month.
+ **Waxing Moon.** The added light calls for action. You are being signaled to put some energy behind those intentions you set

during the new moon. Take steps to show yourself and the universe that you honor your intentions with real-life grit.

✦ **Full Moon.** The intensity of the lunar light during this time can heighten your anxiety and self-awareness. There is no hiding from the work you have put in to honor your intentions in this cycle. The shadows are exposed, and the things you know no longer serve you—things that hinder your progress—need to be released. Write down what you want to let go of on a piece of paper and burn this paper under the light of the full moon.

✦ **Waning Moon.** There can be grief in letting go of what has been with you so long, even though it isn't needed anymore. This cycle allows you to restore balance to your being. Your work is to become comfortable with this new version of you. Use this time to tie up any loose ends to satisfy your intentions as you prepare for the next lunar cycle to begin.

GETTING READY

Most calendars have moon cycles on them, but if not, make notes of the moon phases somewhere you will see them daily. The activities you do for each moon cycle don't have to be time consuming, just consistent. The more you get comfortable linking your personal development to the moon's cycle, you will find yourself with increased self-awareness, personal responsibility, and peace.

With the knowledge of which cycle you are approaching and what the general goals and objectives for that cycle are, create your own life goals that coincide. Journal about what has changed for you since the last cycle and where you see yourself needing to go in the future. Have any helpful crystals and mystical protection tools on hand as well to assist you for the ritual you are about to do. The activities "Program a Crystal" and "Organize and Use Mystical Protection Tools" can assist you with this! If possible, find a spot outside so you can view the moon during this practice. If not, sitting near a window and connecting with nature in that way will also work.

How to Get In Touch with the Moon

1. Use the script in Part 1 or your preferred method to get into a meditative state.
2. Using the information provided earlier in this activity, complete a ritual for the phase of the moon that you are currently in. Pay special attention to how it feels to plant an intention, take action toward that goal, release something you do not need, or wrap things up before the next lunar cycle.

TRY IT OUT

Follow the steps described to get in touch with the moon, completing this practice at least once for each moon phase. Record your answers to these questions to reflect on your experience:

✦ What was my intention this past new moon?
✦ How did I take steps toward it in the waxing moon?
✦ What did I find I needed to release this full moon?
✦ What did I do to balance myself moving forward in the waning moon?
✦ After a full cycle of following the moon's patterns, how do I feel?

35 Connect to Past Lives

Have you ever found yourself in a place that you've never been before, but it felt eerily like home? Do you have a totally random affinity for a culture that you've never been part of or a time period you've always felt drawn and connected to? These are signals of a past life connection! There is a belief that our souls do not spend just one lifetime on this earth plane; rather, we spend many lifetimes within different bodies, experiencing life in a plethora of ways. Energy passing through the eons carries with it energetic memories; past lives are carried with us in subtle frequencies. They appear in our apparently disconnected passions or our intense fascinations. They show up in people who are "new" to us in this lifetime but in actuality are part of our soul family— the special energies that travel with us throughout the ages.

You can connect to your past lives to gain insight and sometimes even closure. For example, a seemingly arbitrary phobia can be a remnant of a past life trauma. Or a pattern in life you find hard to break can indicate a lesson that wasn't quite learned in another lifetime. There are a multitude of ways to create a connection to a past life and to reveal an important energetic memory. You can perform past life connections on your own by paying attention to the seemingly subtle ways you already connect!

GETTING READY

Pay close attention to your thoughts as you are researching seemingly disconnected passions, hobbies, or locations you find yourself interested in. Old perspectives from your past mindset may arise. Perhaps you suddenly feel you are in a mindset that mimics a different personality. In any lifetime, you were a construct of that particular culture, period, and environment. Therefore, a very common past life memory occurrence is to feel as if you are listening to another person's mindset as though it is your own. You may look at certain items of clothing, tools for cooking or a trade, or money and inherently understand when and how they were used in a past life.

Check Your Emotions

You may find yourself impassioned about things that surprise you. Certain events you read about may truly upset you. The history of these things will become alive to you, and feelings of being present will awaken.

After determining a past life connection, bring some of its symbolism, artifacts, and information into your present life. Pictures of architecture, clothing, and items from that time are all useful. You can acquire books and articles discussing the nuances of what fascinates you about that time. Collecting these items, representations, and information that feels aligned with a past life will allow you to more readily connect. The more you throw yourself into these interests, the more their vibrations will start to create visions and past life memories.

As you throw yourself into the everyday artifacts and collected research of this past time, create moments to test yourself. If you find yourself inexplicably connected to an area of the world, visualize where important landmarks would be on a map. If you are feeling aligned to a certain time, look at unfamiliar clothing from today and see if you inherently know how it was to be styled and for what occasions. If a certain religion or culture stands out to you, try to intuitively pick up on traditions, rules, or an overall psyche of that time and see if it checks out when you do more research.

How to Connect to Your Past Lives

1. Once you have done your research and are feeling connected to a certain time, get into a meditative state using the script in Part 1 or your preferred method.
2. Ask your spirit guides to show you glimpses of your old life.
3. In response, you may see this life from your own eyes, a perspective that would be your own. It will feel as if you are going through it, through your own mind and eyes, yet are very detached with an awareness that this isn't *exactly* you. In other words, you are a different version of yourself.
4. When you have these sudden visualizations, try to pick up as much detail as you can. They often come in quick, sudden flashes, layered with emotions and mindsets that are complex. Absorb them, but save their dissection for later.
5. Immediately after getting glimpses, write down anything you can about the details.
6. Research your findings to gain insight and answers about this past life.

TRY IT OUT

Follow the steps described to connect to your past lives. Record your answers to these questions to reflect on your experience:

✦ What interests do I have that feel disconnected to my present life?
✦ How do I feel when I see something that centers around these interests?
✦ When connecting to past life memories, what did I see?
✦ Did I see, hear, or intuit any names during this practice?
✦ What details did I see?

36 Organize and Use Mystical Protection Tools

You will find that while you are able to practice your psychic skill set anywhere, you may come to prefer a quiet and set place devoted to these activities. Using mystical protection tools will not only create a comfortable spot for you to work in but also decrease the environmental variables (e.g., electromagnetic interruptions from computers, social interactions) that can interrupt your spiritual flow. Setting up this space with ample energetic protection and limited interruption will ensure that your energy stays stable and secure when you are in your most vulnerable moments of growth.

Mystical protection tools are there to assist you and create a feeling of comfort and calmness. The more at ease you feel in a consistent space conducive to your psychic practice, the more you will be open to those nudges from Spirit. In your own spiritual journey, you will find items that uniquely celebrate and support you. However, a few staples are necessary for any psychic's tool kit, especially when still in the earlier stages of this journey.

GETTING READY

After selecting a space that feels comfortable to you, it's time to stock it with some mystical protection tool staples. You can gather items that are generalized at first, including:

- **White Candles.** When working in the realms of Spirit, a white candle is a fundamental necessity. Candles can be chosen in different colors for many different reasons, but a white candle calls for the purest spiritual protection you need to bless your space. As you light it before a psychic practice, you can say something to the effect of "I invite the white light of the universe to bless this space." The intention here is to create a neutral and positive high-vibrational workspace that respects and protects your Higher Self.

- **Crystals.** Crystals are thought to protect and hold energy. You will want your programmed crystals near you in your psychic space, as well as others that represent protection from unwanted energetic vibrations. Great protective crystals to start with include rose quartz (promotes self-love, releasing the past, and healing old emotional wounds), amethyst (helps control anxiety and protect from others' intentions), obsidian (blocks psychic attacks, protects energy, and transmutes negative energy into positive energy), and selenite (cleans your aura and cleans and recharges other crystals with a touch). See the "Choose a Crystal for Psychic Work" activity for more guidance. Along the way, your own intuition will lead you to crystals that are uniquely adept in assisting your individual needs.

- **Salt Lamp.** There is a belief that negative ions can elevate our serotonin levels, causing us to feel more energized, positive, and inspired. It is thought that salt lamps can produce negative ions with water particles in the air as the particles evaporate off the heated salt stone.

- **Room Spray.** Many times, the vibrations in a space or your own aura can become stagnant or stressful. Sprays infused with essential oils, salt, or herbs can alleviate the heaviness that comes from backlogged vibrations. To create your own spray, add about 1½ ounces of distilled water and ½ ounce of witch hazel to a 2-ounce spray bottle. Add ten drops of an essential oil that speaks to you. Some great scents include lavender (calms and guards against negativity), frankincense (raises your energetic vibrations and protects), lemon (naturally cleanses your vibration, allowing for space to grow), and cedar (removes fears and blockages and creates fortitude and strength to begin anew). Also feel free to add a few little crystals that you feel bring some spiritual potency to your mix!

As you start using the space and these basic tools, you can look to what your specific needs are to make any nuanced changes. You will receive a lot of feedback from your spirit guides and Higher Self, which will clue you into what you specifically need. Everyone has strengths and weaknesses in their energy fields, things they are working on and places they need some further support. Your intuitive self will receive these messages, and your job will be to listen to their subtle pulls toward gathering more tools that fit your individualized practice. These could include special incense scents, colorful candles, and singing bowls of metal or crystal.

How to Use Your Mystical Tools

1. Gather the general tools for your mystical protection tool kit, placing them in a sacred space devoted to your continued psychic practice.
2. Create a consistent routine of performing your psychic activities, exercises, and meditations in this space.
3. Move your tools around as you intuitively see fit and add more tools that you connect to as time goes on.

TRY IT OUT

Follow the steps described to use mystical tools in a psychic practice. Record your answers to these questions to reflect on your experience:

✦ What types of crystals do I feel attracted to for my tool kit?
✦ When have I felt I needed some protection from others' energies? Why?
✦ What did it feel like to set up these protective energies?
✦ How do I feel in my space when surrounded by my mystical protection tools?
✦ Is there anything else I feel the need to add to my tool kit?

37 Remove Negative Attachments

When we meet and interact with any object, person, or experience, an energy exchange occurs. Every time we have this exchange, a "cord" is formed. Cords are energetic connections created between yourself and events from the past, cultural systems, people, and sometimes objects. When these cords embody love, friendship, and goodness, they are a positive connection. When they hold selfishness, greed, and bad intentions, they are a negative connection. Positive cord attachments feel like intimate and profound connections that bring you joy, a feeling of connectedness, and spiritual evolution. Negative cord attachments feel draining and energetically dim and bring about emotions like jealousy, anger, and spite. Following positive or negative feelings down to their root cause will be how you find the cords you hold.

Negative cords can become unbearable after breakups, a fight with a friend, a sour interaction, a major illness, a job change, whenever anything legal is happening, and anytime you are starting over in life. Fortunately, you can remove these cords.

It is important to note that only *you* can remove your negative cords. The reason the cords exist in the first place is because you found them valuable enough to bind yourself to them. Removing the cords that no longer serve you is a part of the psychic process that centers on self-help and self-awareness.

GETTING READY

The goal in removing a cord is not to remove the memory of what happened; rather, it is to remove the ongoing trauma and suffering that memory causes you. You will want to remove the attachment but keep the lesson(s) you gained from that experience. To prepare for removing a cord, you will need to become aware of what the cord is, how it came about, how it has served you, and why it still lingers. It is also important to reflect on what it taught you. Salvaging that part of the connection is a necessary piece of the ritual to remove the cord.

Also, keep in mind that you will not be "cutting" the cord; you will be removing it. Think of these cords as plants with roots. When you cut a plant but leave the roots, it grows stronger. The removal of the roots is the image you will need to have in your third eye before you begin the practice itself. (See more on the third eye and the other chakras in the "Open Your Third Eye" and "Balance Your Chakras" activities.)

How to Remove Negative Cords

1. Begin in a meditative state (using the script in Part 1 or your preferred method), highly aware of and envisioning what cord you want to remove and why.
2. Visualize your auric bubble, which you learned about in the "Create a Protection Bubble" activity, swelling around you, surrounding your body.
3. Close your eyes and hold your hands up in front of you. Starting at the very top of your head, at your crown chakra, very slowly move your hands downward. As you move your hands, visualize them moving through each chakra. Pay attention to any point where the energy around your hands feels stuck or you have an intrinsic need to spend more time over a certain chakra. Take a mental note of which chakras you stopped at and what they signify.
4. After this chakra scan, visualize the sources of your cord attachment in front of you. Say what you have to say to them. For example, you may say, "I release you with love and light!"
5. Now simply let the cord go. Visualize it dissolving inside of you.

6. Envision the white light of Source, the highest-power universal and benevolent energy that surrounds us all, filling this hole that the cord has left inside you. Take your time with this step.

7. When you feel ready, you may end the meditation with steady breathing and by slowly bringing yourself back to awareness of the physical world around you.

Check Your Emotions

You may feel discomfort during this activity—this is normal! Feeling a little anxious or uncomfortable can be a side product of cord removal. After the cord is removed, you may even feel sad. This cord has been a part of you for some time, and now it is gone. It's okay to grieve your loss while also understanding that it had to go so as to serve your highest good.

The removal of cords and attachments is something you will have to do periodically throughout your psychic journey. It's like weeding a garden; the job is never quite over! It can become easier to do as you practice. After this exercise, repeating a mantra such as "I am filled with light" or "I am completely myself" can be helpful to move forward when you feel scattered or stuck for the next few hours or even days.

TRY IT OUT

Follow the steps described to remove negative cords. Record your answers to these questions to reflect on your experience:

✦ What is the source of one cord I practiced removing?
✦ Which chakras, if any, did I find myself stuck on and why?
✦ What surprised me most about removing my negative cord?

38 Visualize the Immediate Future

As discussed in the "Use Your Psychic Calendar" activity, the future is not a sure thing. We are on trajectories based on our current patterns, choices, and actions. When we shift any of these, our future shifts as well, especially in the short term. It's very much like mapping a path on water; unlike a road map, it will always be different simply because it's not static. However, visualizing the immediate future is something you can do with a lot of veracity. Many of us don't change our patterns, choices, or actions that often; therefore, this exercise can yield pretty accurate results. This exercise can be more trustworthy than predicting the long-term future because our immediate actions are often coming at us with more fervor than the long-term results of our actions and patterns.

You have probably already been doing this in your life. It's often easier with events that you are not that emotionally con-nected to, and you could have been passing it off as common sense instead of a psychic premonition. Knowing that your child will have a good day at school even though they dread going or that a friend will land the job they are interviewing for today is just one example of visualizing the future. You can see yourself celebrating with your friend after they happily announce they got the job. Visualizing the future is about asking yourself what happens next and seeing what reality comes up.

GETTING READY

Start with an event or occurrence that has a short timeline and doesn't have an emotional pull on you: an outcome of a job interview, a move, or a result of an upcoming blind date. Beginning with visualizing the immediate future for someone else is a good place to start. As you get more used to the feelings associated with visualizing, you can begin including yourself in the activity.

You will be visualizing what happens after whatever short-term situation you've chosen. Thinking about the cause of the current situation will be the key to this visualization. You're thinking about all the tiny and little ways life would look different if the thing you are wanting to predict did or did not happen. Visualizing ahead—really putting yourself in the situation of seeing the future—will assist you in this.

Perhaps your friend is going on a blind date this week. They want to know if it's going to go well or not. Instead of focusing on the date itself, focus on your friend. Prepare questions to ask yourself about the future that would clue you into what happened on the date. For this example, helpful questions are:

✦ Do you find them to be happy the next time you see them?
✦ What is the tone and mood of your conversation?
✦ Do you see them texting you that it was a good date or a bad one, or perhaps just a mediocre one? What feelings do you feel when you visualize this future?
✦ Are they busy the following weekend with this new person, or are you still going out together as singles?

The more detailed you can get, the better. Think of lots of questions that would give you a clue to what happened during the date and whether things will shift in the future because of it.

If there is a doctor's appointment, ask yourself about the mood as you walk out the door. If there is a question about how long a project will take, ask yourself if you will be available to go on a vacation the weekend after or not. If you are not sure if a person in your life is going to stay with you or not, try to visualize the next upcoming holiday. Are they with you? Do your family members ask where they are? The emotions you get about the future will tell you what has happened. Reading future feelings is crucial.

How to Perform a Visualization of the Future

1. Begin in a meditative state, using the script in Part 1 or your preferred method.
2. Start to visualize a mundane moment in the very near future, after whatever circumstance in question has already passed. Put yourself in a normal routine or conversation with the person you want to visualize the future for.
3. Ask yourself your list of questions out loud. Add more questions as you feel necessary. Pay close attention to the mood, tone, and emotions you are feeling as you ask the questions and visualize the future. They are messages that carry insight for your vision.
4. When you feel that you have a definitive vision of the future outcome, you can release the visualization.

TRY IT OUT

Follow the steps described to visualize the future. Record your answers to these questions to reflect on your experience:

+ What was the short-term event?
+ What feelings did you have about this event right away when doing the visualization practice?
+ Which questions did you find most helpful in your self-examination of the future?
+ What emotions do you have after visualizing this future?

ACTIVITY

39 Psychically Interpret Handwriting

Do you find yourself intrigued by old letters, cards, or other writings from the past? Ever see a letter written a long time ago and wonder about the person who wrote it? Are you someone who prefers a handwritten note over an email? These are all cues indicating a natural ability toward the psychic skill of reading handwriting!

When someone sits down to write, they do so with an intention. Any piece of writing you find will be filled with a desire to communicate something strongly. Of course, the intention isn't always as clear as the words written on the paper; you may only have their signature in the back of a book to work with. Luckily, the actual words you see are not as important as the intention you will pick up on. Anytime someone records their words, a piece of themselves is left to linger there, to communicate with the reader. This is the energy you will contact in this exercise.

GETTING READY

This gift can take some time to cultivate. It's necessary to use your third eye, so you will want to hone your skill in the "Open Your Third Eye" exercise beforehand.

Apart from opening your third eye, the most important part of this exercise is finding a piece of writing that you are naturally interested in to interpret. Perhaps you have an old family Bible with names written in the back or a love letter penned by an ancestor. Whatever your subject matter, make sure it's intriguing to you. The practice works best when you don't know

238 The Psychic Workbook

much about who wrote it but still have access to information that can confirm what you interpreted. To get better at this skill, you'll need to check your work!

The handwriting can be from someone living or deceased. The messages you receive will be different though, depending on which of these options you choose. If the writing is by someone who has crossed over, you will get a strong connection from them and the energy they have left behind on this earth plane. You may see them with your third eye and be able to describe them. They can show you the room they were writing it in and what they were doing that day. It's like a snapshot of the past. If you are related to this person or are doing this activity for someone who has a similar connection, you can get spirit messages channeled through you. In fact, this is a way to practice mediumship, or communication with those who have crossed over.

If the writer is still living, you are going to receive emotions and intentions from the energy they had at the time of writing. You can get images and feelings about their motives and personalities; you may even be able to see them in your third eye. You can receive information about their journeys happening then and now and overall messages about them as a person. Some psychics will interpret handwriting samples from a person simply to help better connect to their energy.

Above all else, make sure you are curious, since that is the main component to being successful in this endeavor. Once you have your piece of handwriting, you are ready to begin!

How to Psychically Interpret Handwriting

1. In a quiet space, get into a meditative state using the script in Part 1 or your preferred method.
2. Sit with your handwriting sample for a minute. Breathe slowly and steadily, tuning in to the energy of the writing until you feel on the same level as the vibrations being emitted from it.

3. Close your eyes and lightly draw one finger across the hand-writing. Do this slowly, line by line. If you want to repeat and go over a line, that's fine. As you do this, explore with your third eye. Flashes of the past may come in quickly. Do not dismiss them. Simply be curious about what you see and interpret.
4. If you are with someone who can confirm to you who wrote this piece and other information about it, start describing what you see out loud. Their job is to say "yes" or "not quite" or "I don't know." Or you may want them to just record what you write silently, so you can reflect after the practice.
5. When you intuitively feel you are losing the connection and that your practice is done, thank the energy out loud for its participation with your exercise.

TRY IT OUT

Follow the steps described to psychically interpret handwriting. Record your answers to these questions to reflect on your experience:

+ What piece of writing did I choose and what did I feel when choosing it?
+ Do I have an overall intention for this piece? Why?
+ Did I see anything while performing this interpretation? Smell anything? Taste or hear anything?
+ What emotions came up?
+ What message came through during this activity?

40 Understand and Shift Your Energy

When a day starts off on a bad note, the energy will match this low vibration as the day continues. Perhaps you spill your coffee all over your clean shirt, rush out the door, and stub your toe in the process. You find yourself in the car with no gas, only to wait forever for an available pump at the gas station. You hit every red light and are late to work. You can feel your mood sour more and more and almost expect the next bad thing to happen for you. In these moments, you are creating your reality. Like attracts like. Luckily, you aren't a helpless bystander in this negative energy cycle. You can change your entire vibe.

As you become more attuned to your own energy and the energy of the world around you, you'll notice when things don't feel aligned. It can feel uncomfortable and chaotic. You can feel as if you are stuck in a bubble far away from any calm and safe energy. You can find yourself experiencing days—or weeks or even months—of cyclical energy that keeps you down. Noticing these loops of energy that are drawing you in and taking control over your energy output is the first step to changing your direction, not only for the day, but for your life moving forward.

GETTING READY

When you are on an energetic loop of low vibration, first you need to notice it. You need to observe your reality and take note of where you are mentally, spiritually, and emotionally. In the "Sense Someone Else's Feelings" activity, you learned how to create a three-word journal in order to identify your feelings in any given moment. After completing that activity, reflect on the similarities between what you are feeling and the events of the day. This can point to how external vibrations are currently impacting your own energy and how your day unfolds.

How to Understand and Shift Your Energy

1. After identifying your feelings in this exact moment, enter into a meditative state using the script in Part 1 or your preferred method.

2. Visualize loops of energy swirling around you. They may be different sizes, colors, and frequencies. Simply observe them. Notice how they interact or stay separate. These are your energy loops. They may be moving fast or slow; they may be many or few. You may notice them having different colors (you may want to refer back to the activity "Assign Colors to a Situation"), and you may notice some of them feeling more anxious than others. You can move them around, make them larger or smaller, or push them away completely. These loops change all the time.

3. With your intuition, choose the loop you find yourself stuck in today and mindfully notice it. The loop of energy you will find yourself stuck in is the one closest to you and the one you feel the most drawn to in your visualization. It represents an emotion that goes deeper than the present moment. For example, it's possible that the feeling of being rushed is triggering you today because you feel spread too thin. This feeling is what is represented in that frenzied, faded loop you see in your visualization.

4. Once you have focused on a loop and identified the emotions within it, visualize this loop expanding and becoming more abundantly helpful to you in your daily life. Perhaps you see it as

a color you associate with anxiety or dread. Visualize it settling into a color you find more calming. If it is moving frantically, envision it becoming a calmer source of energy instead.

5. You may intuitively feel the need to reach out and touch the loop in your mind's eye and even with your actual hands in the physical world. Do anything that feels natural to you in order to gain control over these energetic loops and move them in ways you inherently know will better your flow. Keeping in mind the feelings you identified in step three will allow you to hone in on the layers of energy that are causing your energetic disruptions.

6. Take a few moments to sit in the quietness of your mind, knowing that you have control over which vibrations you choose to absorb and which you send away.

TRY IT OUT

Follow the steps described to understand and shift your energy. Record your answers to these questions to reflect on your experience:

+ What feelings did I identify before performing this energy shift?
+ How do I feel my reality has been mirroring my feelings?
+ How did I feel immediately upon entering my meditative state?
+ What did I see in my visualization?
+ What did I feel as I visualized the loops of energy?
+ How did I experience the energy visually, physically, spiritually, etc.?
+ How did those sensations change after I performed a calming practice?

Index

Affirmations, 124–25. *See also* Mantras

Ancestors. *See also* Loved ones
contacting, 25
in dreams, 158
emotions and, 156–60
handwriting by, 238–39
lineage of, 173
messages from, 20–21, 25, 156–60
photos of, 16, 29–30, 156–60
psychic bonds with, 156–60
traditions and, 178

Ancestral photos, 16, 29–30, 156–60

Angel numbers
connecting to, 24, 26, 37
interpreting, 18, 197–201
meanings of, 197–99

Angels. *See also* Spirit guides
clear smelling and, 103
connecting to, 24, 26, 37, 77–81, 197–98
ego voice and, 26
explanation of, 24
numbers and, 18, 24, 26, 37, 197–201

Animals
animal messengers, 172–76
art and, 172
communicating with, 172–76, 207–11
lost animals, 87
observing, 188
paranormal activity and, 188
pets, 87, 188, 207–11
symbols and, 172–76

Art
animals in, 172
channeling Spirit in, 113–17
creating, 69
in nature, 69

Astral body, 166–68

Astral projection, 166–71

Astral realm, 166–67

Auras
appearance of, 43, 57–58, 92–97
auric bubble, 229
color of, 92–97
emotions and, 92–97
energy of, 92–95
looking for, 43, 92–97
reading, 92–95
of self, 57–58

Authenticity, 40, 135–36, 202–203

Automatic drawing, 113–15

Automatic writing, 118–23

Balance, achieving, 16, 61–69

Blessings, 177–81, 189

Body
astral body, 166–68
balance for, 16, 61–69
protection bubble for, 16, 56–60, 203, 229
self-care for, 18, 61–66
shadow pains in, 29, 143, 208
spirit shivers and, 25

Boundaries, creating, 130, 202

Calendars
creating, 162–63
moon cycles on, 213
psychic calendar, 28, 161–65, 184, 233–34
three-word journal and, 52
timelines and, 161, 184, 234
using, 28, 161–65, 184, 233

Candles, 178–79, 223–24

Celestial beings, 82, 103. *See also* Angels; Spirit guides

Centering techniques
implementing, 15

Centering techniques—*continued*
    for meditation, 20, 35–38
    for psychic practice, 15, 20, 35–38
Chakras
    balancing, 16, 61–68
    blocked chakras, 61–64
    colors of, 61–63
    crown chakra, 57, 63–64, 229
    explanation of, 16, 61
    heart chakra, 37, 62, 64
    root chakra, 61, 63
    sacral chakra, 62, 64
    scanning, 228–29
    solar plexus chakra, 62, 64
    third eye chakra, 27–28, 41–45, 58, 62–64,
        78, 83–97, 104–5, 132, 141–42, 152–63,
        189, 208, 229, 238–40
    throat chakra, 62, 64, 104, 142
Channeling techniques, 113–23, 156–60,
    238–40
Clairalience, 29–30, 103–7, 208–9
Clairaudience, 28, 98–102
Claircognizance, 29
Clairgustance, 30, 208–9
Clairsentience, 28–29, 51–55, 208
Clairvoyance, 27–28
Cleansings, 177–81, 189
Cold readings, 137
Colors
    assigning, 192–96
    of auras, 92–97
    of chakras, 61–63
    of crystals, 151–52
    emotions and, 92–97
    for healing, 93
    of protection tools, 223
    psychic readings and, 194
    seeing, 41–45, 92–97, 192–96
Communication. *See also* Messages
    with ancestors, 20–21, 25, 156–60
    with animals, 172–76, 207–11
    healing communication, 204
    improving, 15, 35
    with loved ones, 20–21, 25, 30, 103,
        156–60
    with pets, 207–11
    with Spirit, 35, 57, 82–83
    telepathy, 16, 22, 28, 108–12, 202–204

Cord attachments, 228–32
Creative voice, 26–27
Crystals
    choosing, 130–34
    colors of, 151–52
    desire and, 152–53
    emotions and, 151–55
    frequencies of, 151–53, 223
    healing with, 151–55
    love and, 151
    programming, 151–55, 223
    protective crystals, 130, 152, 223
    for psychic work, 130–34, 151–55

Desires
    crystals and, 152–53
    ego and, 33
    intentions and, 34–35
    letting go of, 33
    manifesting, 20, 87–91, 124–29
Distant realms, 98–102
Divine messengers, 20–21. *See also* Spirit
Drawing, automatic, 113–15
Dreams
    ancestors in, 158
    astral travel and, 166–67
    interpreting, 72–76, 109, 158
    lucid dreams, 167
    recording, 167
    repetitive dreams, 74
    symbols in, 73–74
    telepathy via, 109
    types of, 72–73, 167
    typical dreams, 167

Earth
    connecting with, 67–71
    earth plane, 24, 27, 41, 63, 77, 217, 239
    grounding techniques, 67–71, 151
Ego
    desire and, 33
    intentions and, 34–35, 126
    intuition and, 26, 32–33
    judgment and, 32–33
    meditation and, 35–36
    self-doubt and, 32–33
    understanding, 26, 32–33
Ego voice, 26, 32

Emotional conduit, 51–53
Emotional energies, 51–53, 243–47
Emotional healing, 151–52, 223
Emotional intuition, 18
Emotional wounds, 31, 174, 223
Emotions
    ancestors and, 156–60
    auras and, 92–97
    balancing, 61–66
    colors and, 92–97
    crystals and, 151–55
    loved ones and, 156–60
    objects and, 141–45
    palm readings and, 146–50
    paranormal activity and, 187–91
    pets and, 207–11
    psychic readings and, 146–50
    scanning, 46–53, 136, 143
    sensing, 28–29, 51–55, 119, 208
Energy. See also Frequencies
    of auras, 92–95
    authentic energy, 40, 135–36, 202–203
    celestial energy, 82
    cords of, 228–32
    of crystals, 151–53, 223
    currents of, 21, 46–50
    cyclical energy, 212–14, 243–47
    emotional energies, 51–53, 243–47
    in environment, 46–50, 187–88
    grounding, 67–71, 151
    interpreting, 15–16, 34–35, 141–45
    life-force energy, 92–95
    loops of, 243–47
    of moon, 212–16
    of objects, 141–45
    observing, 17–18, 243–47
    of pictures, 135–40
    reading, 17–18
    scanning, 46–53
    sending away, 202–206
    shifting, 243–47
    tapping into, 34–35
    telepathic energy, 108–12, 202–206
    understanding, 15–16, 243–47
    of universe, 21–22, 34–35, 167, 197, 223
Environment
    energy in, 46–50, 187–88
    frequencies in, 187–88

scanning, 46–53
Essential oils, 104, 178, 223–24
Exercises, 39–247
Extrasensory perception, 87

Fear, overcoming, 15, 31–35, 168, 174, 224
Feelings, sensing, 28–29, 51–55, 119, 208. See
    also Emotions
Frequencies. See also Energy
    of crystals, 151–53, 223
    in environment, 187–88
    interpreting, 15–16, 34–35, 141–45
    observing, 243–47
    in past lives, 217
    understanding, 15–16
Future
    changing, 161–62
    goals for, 213–14
    immediate future, 233–37
    long-term future, 182–86, 233
    premonitions of, 161–62, 182–86, 233
    short-term future, 233–37
    visualizing, 233–37

Goals. See also Intentions
    achieving, 77, 130, 151, 213–14
    aligning, 21–22, 213–14
    for future, 213–14
    higher consciousness goal, 22
Gratitude, 38, 42, 68, 110, 125–26, 156
Grounding techniques, 67–71, 151

Handwriting, 238–42
Healing
    balance for, 61–66
    blessings and, 177
    colors for, 93
    crystals for, 151–55
    emotional healing, 151–52, 223
    healing communication, 204
    healing journey, 31
    healing light, 36, 57, 167
    self-care for, 61–66
    spirit guides for, 82–86
    spiritual healing, 24
    of wounds, 31, 174, 223
Herbs, 178–79, 223–24
Higher Self. See also Spirit guides

Higher Self—*continued*
   astral projection and, 166–71
   connecting to, 21–27, 72–74, 82, 108–12,
     118–19, 166–71
   creative voice and, 26–27
   ego voice and, 26
   explanation of, 21–27
   intuition and, 58
   messages from, 25–26, 28, 35, 113–14, 224
   protecting, 223
   psychic senses and, 27–32
   sensing, 24–25, 28
   spirit shivers and, 25
House, blessing, 177–81, 189
House, cleansing, 177–81, 189

Insecurities, 47, 61, 73, 207–9
Insight
   channeling Spirit and, 118–19
   dreams and, 72–76
   gaining, 15, 26, 30–31, 40–43, 182–84,
     217–19
   palm readings and, 146–5
   third eye and, 41–43
Inspiration, 18, 78–79, 173
Intentions
   desire and, 34–35
   ego and, 34–35, 126
   manifesting, 21–22, 124–29, 151–55
   mantras for, 124–26
   psychic abilities and, 17, 21–22, 34–35
   reflecting on, 34–35
   setting, 17, 22, 34–35
Intuition
   desire and, 33
   ego and, 26, 32–33
   emotional intuition, 18
   Higher Self and, 58
   judgment and, 32–33
   psychic abilities and, 17–18, 22–23, 40
   self-doubt and, 32–33
   strengthening, 20–21
   tapping into, 17, 20–21, 30–33
   understanding, 17–18
   validation and, 33

Journal
   for animal messages, 173
   for channeling Spirit, 119–20
   of dreams, 72–73, 167
   for energy scan, 47
   for lunar cycles, 212–13
   for memory keeping, 157–60
   in nature, 69
   for palm readings, 146
   for predictions, 182–84
   for symbol book, 82–86
   three-word journal, 52–53, 157, 244
   for tracking progress, 33, 82–86
Judgments, 32–33, 62, 89

Life-force energy, 92–95. *See also* Energy
Long-term future, 182–86, 233
Long-term predictions, 29, 161–62, 182–86
Love
   affirmations for, 124–25
   crystals and, 151
   feeling, 32, 36, 156, 228
   palm readings and, 146–47
   receiving, 62, 77, 147
   self-love, 40, 147, 223
   sending, 108–10, 204
   style of, 147
   true love, 192
   unconditional love, 21, 77, 79, 197
Loved ones. *See also* Ancestors
   clear smelling and, 103
   connecting to, 21–22, 25–30, 141
   contacting, 25–26, 72–73
   in dreams, 158
   ego voice and, 26
   emotions and, 156–60
   messages from, 20–21, 25, 30, 103, 156–60
   psychic senses and, 28–30
   visitations from, 72–73
Lunar cycles, 212–14

Manifestations
   of desires, 20, 87–91, 124–29
   of intentions, 21–22, 124–29, 151–55
   mantras for, 124–26
   power of, 51–52, 124–29, 182–86
Mantras
   for channeling Spirit, 119
   for manifesting intentions, 124–26
   for meditation, 36, 114

for removing negativity, 230
Meditation
    breathing techniques, 37–38
    centering techniques, 20, 35–38
    ego and, 35–36
    for focus, 17
    gratitude during, 38, 68
    interference with, 35–36
    length of, 37
    mantras for, 36, 114
    method for, 35–38
    place for, 35
    position for, 36
    for psychic practice, 17, 20, 35–38
    rituals for, 167
    script for, 37
    steps for, 35–38
Messages. *See also* Communication
    from ancestors, 20–21, 25, 156–60
    from ancestral photos, 156–60
    divining, 18, 20–21
    from Higher Self, 25–26, 28, 35, 113–14,
        224
    from loved ones, 20–21, 25, 30, 103,
        156–60
    from objects, 141–45, 207
    receiving, 15–17, 20–21, 23–27, 35–38,
        141–45, 156–60
    sources of, 20–21, 23–27
    from Spirit, 20–21, 25–26, 28, 31, 57, 69,
        113–23, 184, 224
    from spirit guides, 21, 30, 113–14, 137,
        173–74, 197–201
    from universe, 21, 30
    from unseen realms, 20–21
Messengers
    ancestor messengers, 20–21
    animal messengers, 172–76
    divine messengers, 20–21, 34
Mind
    clearing, 17, 36, 47
    open mind, 15, 33, 40, 79, 131, 135
    subconscious mind, 17–18, 72, 108, 113, 168
Mindfulness, 33, 42, 67–68, 113–15
Moon
    energy of, 212–16
    phases of, 212–14
    ritual with, 212–16

Motivation, 15, 32, 62, 93, 158
Mystical protection tools, 183, 213–14, 222–27.
    See also Protection tools

Nature
    aligning self with, 21, 67–68
    art in, 69
    connecting with, 67–71, 78, 98–102, 172,
        213–14
    journaling in, 69
    studying, 69
Negative attachments, 228–32

Objects, 141–45, 207, 228
Obstacles, 15, 23, 31–33
Open mind, 15, 33, 40, 79, 131, 135

Palm readings
    emotions and, 146–50
    interpreting, 18, 146–50
    lines of palm, 147–48
    love and, 146–47
    performing, 146–50
Paranormal activity, 187–91
Past
    connection to, 16, 187–91, 217–21
    releasing, 31, 223, 228–32
    trauma of, 31, 92, 217
Past life connections, 16, 187–91, 217–21
Patience, 27, 42, 52–53, 79, 120
Perception, changing, 18
Perception, extrasensory, 87
Perspective, changing, 17–18
Perspective, gaining, 82, 166, 194
Pets. *See also* Animals
    communicating with, 207–11
    emotions and, 207–11
    lost pets, 87
    observing, 188
    paranormal activity and, 188
    psychic readings of, 207–11
Photos
    ancestral photos, 16, 29–30, 156–60
    past lives and, 218
    for predictions, 183
    reading, 135–40, 156–60
Physical realm, 24, 27, 41, 187
Physical senses, 27–28, 40, 52

Predictions, 29, 161–62, 182–86
Premonitions, 161–62, 182, 233
Progress
    ego and, 32
    journal of, 33, 82–86
    timeline for, 42
    tracking, 17, 33, 53, 82–86, 213
Protection bubble, 16, 56–60, 203, 229
Protection tools
    candles, 178–79, 223–24
    colors of, 223
    crystals, 130, 152, 223
    mystical protection tools, 183, 213–14,
        222–27
    organizing, 222–27
    protection bubble, 16, 56–60, 203, 229
    for rituals, 213
    using, 222–27
Protective crystals, 130, 152, 223. See also
    Crystals
Psychic abilities
    centering for, 15, 20, 35–38
    developing, 15–18
    exercises for, 17–18, 39–247
    explanation of, 21–23
    focus on, 17–18
    intentions and, 17, 21–22, 34–35
    intuition and, 17–18, 22–23, 40
    maximizing, 15–16
    nurturing, 16–18
    preparing to use, 17–18, 21–23, 34–38
    progress of, 17, 33, 42, 53, 82–86, 213
    reflecting on, 18, 34–35
    strengthening, 15–38, 40, 51, 73
    unique abilities, 16, 20–21, 40
    unlocking, 15
Psychic calendar, 28, 161–65, 184, 213, 233
Psychic gifts
    awakening, 41
    dreams and, 72–76
    senses and, 27–32, 98–107
    strengthening, 15–38, 40, 51, 73
    understanding, 17–22, 40–41
Psychic journey
    beginning, 17, 40
    ego and, 32–33
    importance of, 32–33
    self-care during, 18

unique journey, 16, 40
Psychic practice
    beginning, 17–18, 21–23, 34–38
    centering for, 15, 20, 35–38
    crystals for, 130–34, 151–55, 223
    exercises for, 17–18, 39–247
    meditation for, 17, 20, 35–38
Psychic readings. See also Palm readings
    of ancestral photos, 156–60
    of auras, 92–95
    cold readings, 137
    colors and, 194
    emotions and, 146–50
    palmistry, 18, 146–50
    pet readings, 207–11
    of pictures, 135–40
    predictions and, 182–86
    spirit shivers and, 25
    symbols and, 182–86
Psychic realm, 20–27, 40–41, 151
Psychic senses. See also Senses
    clairalience, 29–30, 103–7, 208–9
    clairaudience, 28, 98–102
    claircognizance, 29
    clairgustance, 30, 208–9
    clairsentience, 28–29, 51–55, 208
    clairvoyance, 27–28
    explanation of, 27–32
    using, 20–21, 27–32
Psychic talents, 15, 40

Realms
    astral realm, 166–67
    distant realms, 98–102
    physical realm, 24, 27, 41, 187
    psychic realm, 20–27, 40–41, 151
    spirit realms, 34, 73, 98, 223
    unseen realms, 20–21
Remote viewing, 87–91, 132
Rituals
    of meditating, 167
    with moon, 212–16
    protection tools for, 213
    for removing negativity, 228–32
Room spray, 223

Salt lamp, 223
Scents, 29–30, 103–7, 178, 208–9, 223–24

Self-awareness, 51–52, 56, 62, 105, 212–13, 228
Self-care, 18, 61–66
Self-confidence, 20–22, 30–32, 40, 62–63, 182
Self-doubt, 15, 20, 32–33
Self-knowledge, 31–33
Self-love, 40, 147, 223
Self-reflection, 34–35
Senses
    physical senses, 27–28, 40, 52, 88, 119
    psychic senses, 27–32, 98–107, 208–9
    remote viewing and, 87–91
    using, 20–21, 27–32, 87–91
Shadow pains, 29, 143, 208
Soul contract, 24, 82, 118
Space, blessing, 177–81, 189
Spirit. See also Spirit guides
    art and, 113–17
    channeling, 113–23
    communication with, 35, 57, 82–83
    creative voice and, 26–27
    divine messengers, 20–21
    ego voice and, 26
    explanation of, 21
    messages from, 20–21, 25–26, 28, 31, 57, 69, 113–23, 184, 224
    psychic senses and, 27–32
    spirit shivers and, 25
    understanding, 21
    voice of, 21
    writing and, 118–23
Spirit guides. See also Angels; Spirit
    connecting to, 24–30, 77–82
    contacting, 77–81
    dreams and, 72–73
    ego voice and, 26
    explanation of, 24, 77–78, 82
    for healing, 82–86
    meeting, 77–81
    messages from, 21, 30, 113–14, 137, 173–74, 197–201
    psychic senses and, 28–30
    symbol book, 82–86, 173
    visitations with, 72–73, 166–68
Spirit realms, 34, 73, 98, 223
Spirit shivers, 25
Spiritual gift, 28, 56, 63, 73
Stress

experiencing, 52, 99, 115, 135–36, 177
    insecurities and, 47, 73
    reducing, 115, 177, 223
    sensing, 47, 192
Subconscious, 17–18, 72, 108, 113, 168
Symbol book, 82–86, 173
Symbols
    ancestors and, 158
    animals and, 172–76
    book of, 82–86, 173
    crystals as, 130
    in dreams, 73–74
    predictions and, 182–86

Telepathic text, 16, 28, 108–12, 202
Telepathy, 16, 22, 28, 108–12, 202–204
Timelines, 42, 157, 161, 184, 234

Universe
    energy of, 21–22, 34–35, 167, 197, 223
    messages from, 21, 30
    protective light of, 167, 223
    understanding, 21–22
Unseen realms, 20–21

Validation, 27, 33, 157, 193
Visions
    creating, 218
    loved ones and, 25
    objects and, 141–43
    protection bubble and, 56–58
    remote viewing, 88
    third eye and, 41–43, 142–43

Workbook exercises, 39–247
Wounds, healing, 31, 174, 223
Writing
    automatic writing, 118–23
    handwriting, 238–42
    Spirit and, 118–23

About the Author

Mystic Michaela is a fourth-generation psychic medium. Her true passion is guiding people through Spirit to live their own authentic lives. Michaela currently resides in South Florida, where she has a thriving practice of personal clients. She is also the host of her own podcast, *Know Your Aura with Mystic Michaela*. She has been featured as a New Age expert in *Well+Good*, *Cosmopolitan*, *Shape*, *Elle*, *Mashable*, *HelloGiggles*, and more.

··· TAP INTO YOUR ···
INNATE ABILITIES!

Here's an amazing fact: You are psychic.

Born with the innate ability to perceive the world uniquely, you were always psychic. And with *The Psychic Workbook*, you can grow and fine-tune your power to experience the world in a whole new way.

This guided workbook will help you unlock your psychic skills to their maximum potential. Inside, find forty step-by-step activities designed to help you strengthen aspects of your abilities. To maintain your psychic growth, you can go through the exercises however many times you need. From opening your third eye to balancing your chakras to receiving messages from ancestral photos, you will be more in touch with yourself and the world around you than ever before.

With the help of *The Psychic Workbook*,
it's time to begin your exciting psychic journey!

MYSTIC MICHAELA is a fourth-generation psychic medium. Her true passion is guiding people through Spirit to live their own authentic lives. Michaela currently resides in South Florida, where she has a thriving practice of personal clients. She is also the host of her own podcast, *Know Your Aura with Mystic Michaela*. She has been featured as a New Age expert in *Well+Good*, *Cosmopolitan*, *Shape*, *Elle*, *Mashable*, *HelloGiggles*, and more.

NEW AGE   0123
ISBN 978-1-5072-2020-7   **$15.99 U.S.**/$21.99 Can.

51599

9 781507 220207

adams media